Singing Bee!

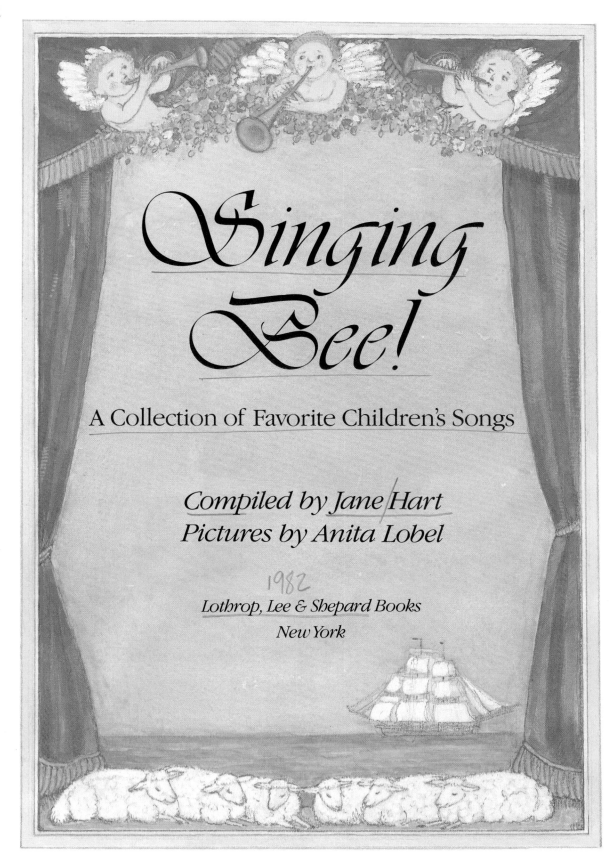

Singing Bee!

A Collection of Favorite Children's Songs

Compiled by Jane Hart
Pictures by Anita Lobel

1982

Lothrop, Lee & Shepard Books
New York

The compiler is grateful to the following for granting permission to include copyrighted material in this collection: Page 11, "All the Pretty Little Horses," collected, adapted, and arranged by John A. Lomax & Alan Lomax TRO, copyright © 1934 and renewed © 1962 by Ludlow Music, Inc., New York, New York, used by permission. Page 77, "Five Little Chickadees," from *The Song Play Book* by Crampton and Wallaston, copyright © 1917 by A.S. Barnes Company. Page 83, "Bluebird," *Sally Go Round the Sun* by Edith Fowke, Copyright © 1969 by McClelland and Stewart Ltd. and reprinted by permission of Doubleday & Company, Inc. Page 84, "The Gallant Ship," from *The Song Play Book* by Crampton and Wallaston, copyright © 1917 by A.S. Barnes Company. Page 86, "Clap Your Hands," from *American Folk Songs for Children* by Ruth Crawford Seeger, copyright © 1948 by Ruth Crawford Seeger, reprinted by permission of Doubleday & Company, Inc. Page 93, "Gogo," by Margaret Marks and Mary Okari, from *Making Music Your Own, Book 2*, copyright ©1971 by General Learning Corporation and reprinted by permission of Silver Burdett Company. Page 97, "Three White Gulls," from Botsford Collection of Folksongs, copyright © 1933 by G. Schirmer, Inc., used by permission. Page 98, "See the Pony Galloping Galloping," composer/arranger, Roberta McLaughlin, Lucille Wood, Jacques Rupp, copyright © 1969 by Bowmar Publishing Corp. and assigned 1981 to Belwin-Mills Pub. Corp., used with permission and all rights reserved. Page 106, "Here Stands a Redbird," from *Sally Go Round the Sun* by Edith Fowke, copyright © 1969 by McClelland and Stewart Ltd. and reprinted by permission of Doubleday & Company, Inc. Page 121, "Roll Over," from *Sally Go Round the Sun* by Edith Fowke, copyright © 1969 by McClelland and Stewart Ltd. and reprinted by permission of Doubleday & Company, Inc. Page 124, "Eletelephony," from *Tirra Lirra* by Laura E. Richards, copyright © 1930, 1932 by Laura E. Richards and used by permission of Little, Brown and Company. Page 130, "The Bus Song," adapted with new music, lyrics, and arrangement, from *Eye Winker, Tom Tinker, Chin Chopper* by Tom Glazer, copyright © 1973 by Songs Music, Inc., Scarborough, New York, used by permission. Page 136, "El Coquito" (The Little Tree Toad), from *Sing a Song with Charity Bailey*, copyright © 1955 by Plymouth Music Co., Inc., New York, New York, used by permission. Page 137, "Mexican Counting Song," from *Children's Songs of Mexico*, copyright © 1963 and used by permission of Highland Music Company. Page 144, "Hanukkah Song," from *Gateway to Jewish Song*, copyright © 1939 by Behrman's Jewish Book House, Inc., and renewed © 1967 by Ginn & Company.

Library of Congress Cataloging in Publication Data
Main entry under title: Singing bee!
Summary: A collection of over one hundred songs, including lullabies, holiday and traditional songs, singing games, and finger plays. 1. Children's songs. 2. Nursery schools — Music. [1. Songs] I. Hart, Jane, (date). II. Lobel, Anita, ill.   M1990.S584   82-15296
ISBN 0-688-41975-5   AACR2

For Daniel, Elizabeth, and Laura

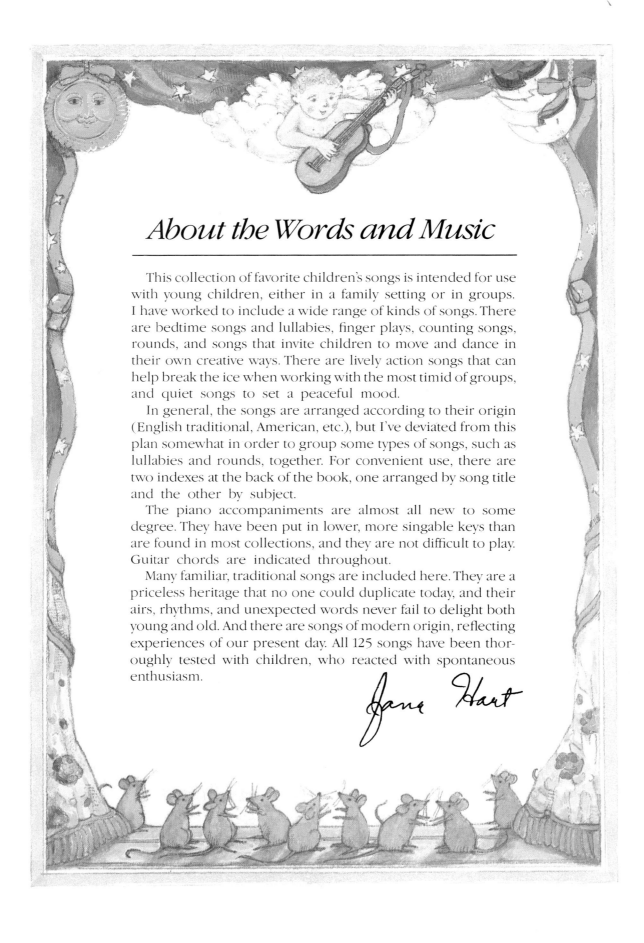

About the Words and Music

This collection of favorite children's songs is intended for use with young children, either in a family setting or in groups. I have worked to include a wide range of kinds of songs. There are bedtime songs and lullabies, finger plays, counting songs, rounds, and songs that invite children to move and dance in their own creative ways. There are lively action songs that can help break the ice when working with the most timid of groups, and quiet songs to set a peaceful mood.

In general, the songs are arranged according to their origin (English traditional, American, etc.), but I've deviated from this plan somewhat in order to group some types of songs, such as lullabies and rounds, together. For convenient use, there are two indexes at the back of the book, one arranged by song title and the other by subject.

The piano accompaniments are almost all new to some degree. They have been put in lower, more singable keys than are found in most collections, and they are not difficult to play. Guitar chords are indicated throughout.

Many familiar, traditional songs are included here. They are a priceless heritage that no one could duplicate today, and their airs, rhythms, and unexpected words never fail to delight both young and old. And there are songs of modern origin, reflecting experiences of our present day. All 125 songs have been thoroughly tested with children, who reacted with spontaneous enthusiasm.

Jane Hart

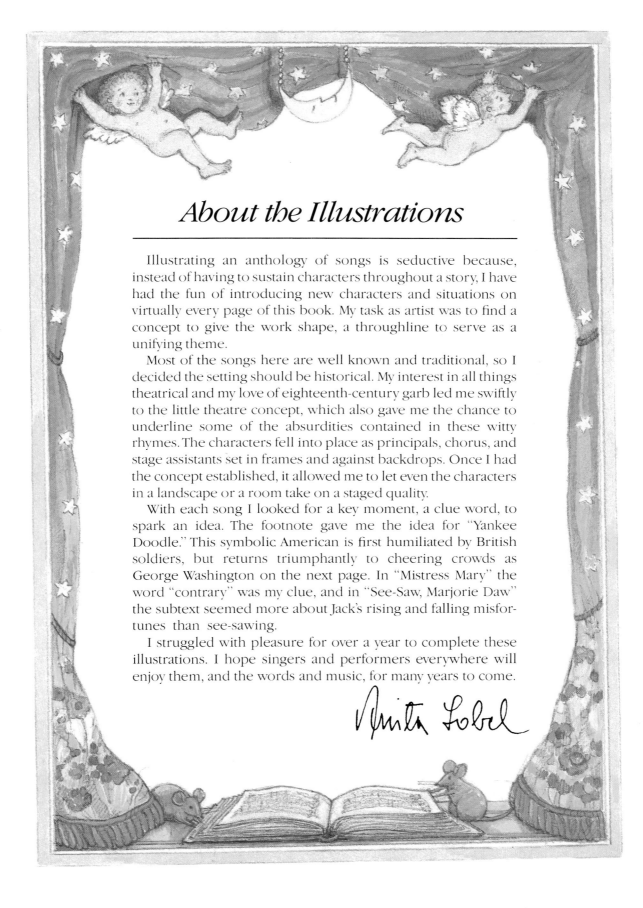

About the Illustrations

Illustrating an anthology of songs is seductive because, instead of having to sustain characters throughout a story, I have had the fun of introducing new characters and situations on virtually every page of this book. My task as artist was to find a concept to give the work shape, a throughline to serve as a unifying theme.

Most of the songs here are well known and traditional, so I decided the setting should be historical. My interest in all things theatrical and my love of eighteenth-century garb led me swiftly to the little theatre concept, which also gave me the chance to underline some of the absurdities contained in these witty rhymes. The characters fell into place as principals, chorus, and stage assistants set in frames and against backdrops. Once I had the concept established, it allowed me to let even the characters in a landscape or a room take on a staged quality.

With each song I looked for a key moment, a clue word, to spark an idea. The footnote gave me the idea for "Yankee Doodle." This symbolic American is first humiliated by British soldiers, but returns triumphantly to cheering crowds as George Washington on the next page. In "Mistress Mary" the word "contrary" was my clue, and in "See-Saw, Marjorie Daw" the subtext seemed more about Jack's rising and falling misfortunes than see-sawing.

I struggled with pleasure for over a year to complete these illustrations. I hope singers and performers everywhere will enjoy them, and the words and music, for many years to come.

Anita Lobel

Guitar Chords

× = Don't play this string

Roman Numerals = fret numbers   •—• = bar with first finger

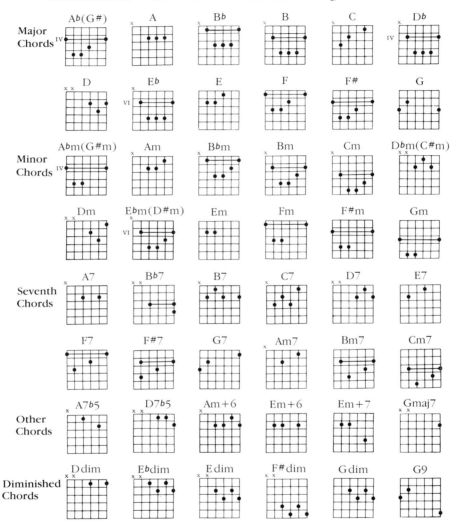

Acknowledgments

Many people contributed to the successful completion of this volume, all of whom deserve a special vote of thanks. My husband, Leslie A. Hart, and my sister Amelia M. Taylor, contributed and helped in many ways. Jamie Williams assisted with the guitar chords. Grace Greene supplied the words to "Hippity Hop to Bed," and William Greene provided the words and music to "Street Song." Helen Wade, Nancy Jaye, Marion Perlov, Lucette Flanagan, Norman Brooks, Felice Biseni, Thyra Sundberg, Sue Raymond, and Genevieve Senber lent irreplaceable copies from their teaching libraries and childhood music book collections.

Three sources proved particularly helpful in making this collection: *The Oxford Nursery Rhyme Book* and *The Oxford Book of Children's Verse* by Iona and Peter Opie (both published by Oxford University Press), and *The Annotated Mother Goose* by William S. Baring-Gould and Ceil Baring-Gould (published by Bramhall House). Reference to these, as well as to other standard sources and a good deal of library hunting, guided decisions on versions of words and music.   J.H

All the Pretty Little Horses

This gentle, beautiful song has long been a well-loved lullaby in the Deep South.

Hush, Little Baby

This engaging song appears to be an old Southern version of a still older traditional English lullaby.

Softly rocking Lullaby

Hush, lit-tle ba-by, don't say a word,

Pa-pa's going to buy you a mock-ing-bird; And

if that mock-ing-bird won't sing,

Pa-pa's going to buy you a dia-mond ring.

1. If that diamond ring turns brass,
Papa's going to buy you a looking glass.
2. If that looking glass gets broke,
Papa's going to buy you a billy goat.
3. If that billy goat won't pull,
Papa's going to buy you a cart and bull.

4. If that cart and bull turns over,
Papa's going to buy you a dog named Rover.
5. If that dog named Rover won't bark,
Papa's going to buy you a horse and cart.
6. If that horse and cart fall down,
You'll still be the sweetest baby in town!

Hippity Hop to Bed

As a going-to-bed song, this is hard to beat.

G. Greene
Casual, at first

J. Hart

Hip - pi - ty hop to bed, _____ I'd rath - er stay up in -

stead. But! When Dad - dy says "must," There's no - thing else, just

Hip - pi - ty, hop - pi - ty, Hip - pi - ty, hop - pi - ty, Hip - pi - ty, hop - pi - ty,

Hip - pi - ty, hip - pi - ty, hop! _____ To bed!

Bye, Baby Bunting

One of the earliest lullabies. "Bunting" was a term of endearment originating in Scotland.

Gently rocking

English Traditional Lullaby

Bye, ba - by bunt - ing, Dad - dy's gone a - hunt - ing, To get a lit - tle rab - bit skin To wrap his ba - by bunt - ing in.

The Sandman Comes

English Traditional Lullaby

Flowing

The sand - man comes, the sand - man comes, He brings such pret - ty snow - white sand, For ev' - ry child through - out the land, The sand - man comes.

Golden Slumbers

Gently rocking

English Traditional Lullaby

Gol - den slum - bers kiss your eyes;

Smiles — a - wake you when you rise; Sleep, pret - ty ba - by,

do — not cry, — And I will sing a lul - la - by,

Rock — then, rock then, lul - la - by. —

Lullaby

Words adapted by L. Hart from the German
Tenderly

Brahms

Lull - a - by, and good night, In the sky stars are bright; Round your head, flow - ers gay Scent your slum - bers till day. Close your eyes now and rest, May these hours be blest, Go to sleep now and rest, May these hours be blest.

Sleep, Baby, Sleep

Gently rocking

English Traditional Lullaby

Sleep, ba - by, sleep, Thy fa - ther guards the sheep, Thy

moth - er shakes the dream - land tree, And from it fall sweet

dreams for thee, Sleep, ba - by, sleep, Sleep, ba - by, sleep. ——

Wee Willie Winkie

English Traditional Lullaby
Adapted by J. Hart

Wee Wil-lie Win-kie runs through the town, Up-stairs, down-stairs,
in his night-gown; Rap-ping at the win-dow, Cry-ing at the lock,
Are the chil-dren all in bed? For now it's eight o'-clock!

19

Rockabye, Baby

Gently

English Traditional Lullaby

Rock - a - bye, ba - by, on the tree top,

When the wind blows, the cra - dle will rock;

When the bough breaks, the cra - dle will fall, And

down will come ba - by, cra - dle and all.

Now the Day Is Over

This lovely old hymn is gentle and soothing, a good lullaby for a tired child.

Sabine Baring-Gould
Softly

Joseph Barnaby
Lullaby

G   D   G   Em   B7   Em

Now the day is o - ver, Night is draw - ing nigh;

A7   D   G   D7   G

R.H. Shad - ows of the eve - ning Steal a - cross the sky.

Father, give the weary
Calm and sweet repose;
With thy tender blessing,
May our eyelids close.

The Caterpillar

Emilie Poulsson
Brightly

Cornelia C. Roeske
English Finger Play

Fuz - zy lit - tle cat - er - pil - lar, Crawl - ing, crawl - ing on the ground, Fuz - zy lit - tle cat - er - pil - lar, No - where, no - where to be found, Tho' we've looked and looked and hunt - ed, Ev - 'ry where a - round!

When the little caterpillar
Found his furry coat too tight,
Then a snug cocoon he made him,
Spun of silk so soft and light;
Rolled himself away within it–
Slept there day and night.

See how this cocoon is stirring–
Now a little head we spy.
What! is this our caterpillar,
Spreading gorgeous wings to dry?
Soon the free and happy creature
Flutters gaily by.

The thumb, hiding in the first, is the caterpillar, and the fist is the cocoon.
Move the thumb in the fist to act out verses one and two. On the third verse,
cross your thumbs and spread fingers wide to indicate the butterfly drying
its wings. Move your fingers and the "happy creature flutters gaily by."

Here Are My Lady's Knives and Forks

J. Hart
English Finger Play

English Traditional Nursery Rhyme

Here are my la - dy's knives and forks, Here is my la - dy's ta - ble; Here is my la - dy's look - ing glass, And here is my ba - by's cra - dle.

For this finger play: Interlock fingers with palms turned up to indicate the knives and forks. Fingers still interlocked, turn palms down, and backs of hands become the table. To suggest the looking glass, form a circle by touching the index fingers and thumbs together. Rest one hand lightly on top of the other, palms up, and rock arms back and forth to make the cradle.

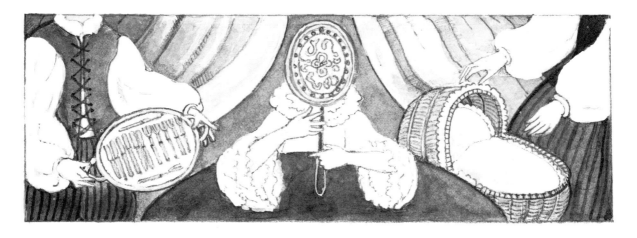

Here Is the Church

English Traditional Nursery Rhyme

J. Hart
English Finger Play

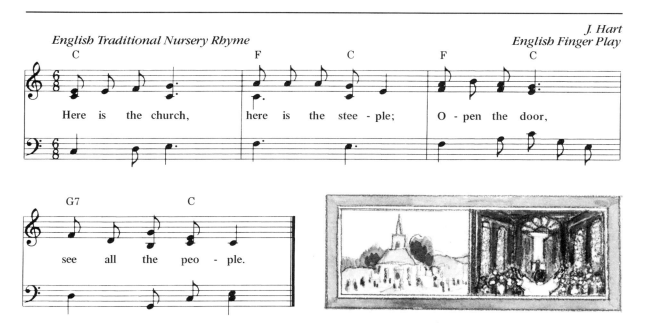

Interlock fingers, down. Raise two index fingers for steeple. Turn fingers up to see all the people—children like to see them in motion, wiggling.

Knock at the Door

English Traditional Nursery Rhyme

J. Hart
English Finger Play

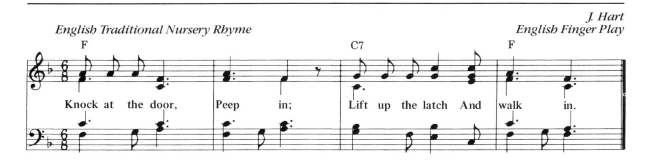

As you sing to a little one, lightly touch his forehead as you sing "Knock at the door." On "Peep in," gently touch the eyelids. On "Lift up the latch" touch the nose, and on "Walk in," touch the baby's mouth.

This Little Pig

English Traditional Song
English Finger Play

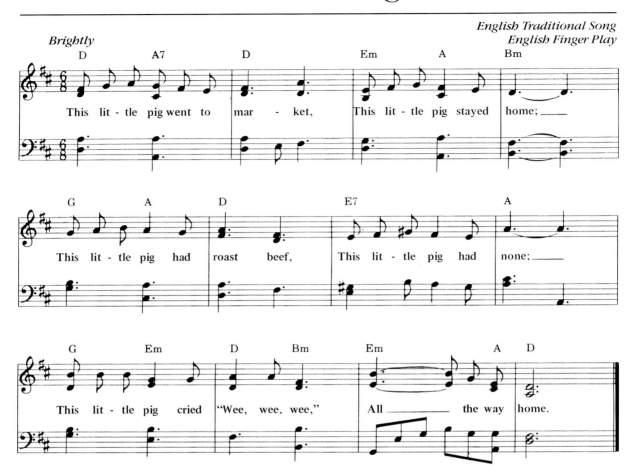

Brightly

This lit - tle pig went to mar - ket, This lit - tle pig stayed home;___

This lit - tle pig had roast beef, This lit - tle pig had none;___

This lit - tle pig cried "Wee, wee, wee," All ___ the way home.

Take hold of the baby's big toe for the first line; then on to the others in turn, reaching the little toe, which is vigorously waggled to "Wee, wee, wee!" You may have to repeat the whole procedure quite a number of times.

Pat-a-Cake

Brightly

English Finger Play

Pat - a - cake, pat - a - cake, ba - ker's man,

Bake me a cake just as fast as you can.

Pat it and shape it and mark it with B,

And bake it in the ov - en for Ba - by and me.

Incey Wincey Spider

Playfully

English Finger Play

The in-cey win-cey spi-der went up the wa-ter spout; Down came the rain and washed the spi-der out; Out came the sun and dried up all the rain, And the in-cey win-cey spi-der went up the spout a-gain.

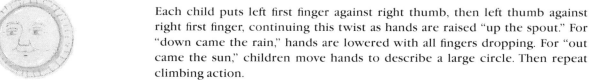

Each child puts left first finger against right thumb, then left thumb against right first finger, continuing this twist as hands are raised "up the spout." For "down came the rain," hands are lowered with all fingers dropping. For "out came the sun," children move hands to describe a large circle. Then repeat climbing action.

Where Is Thumbkin?

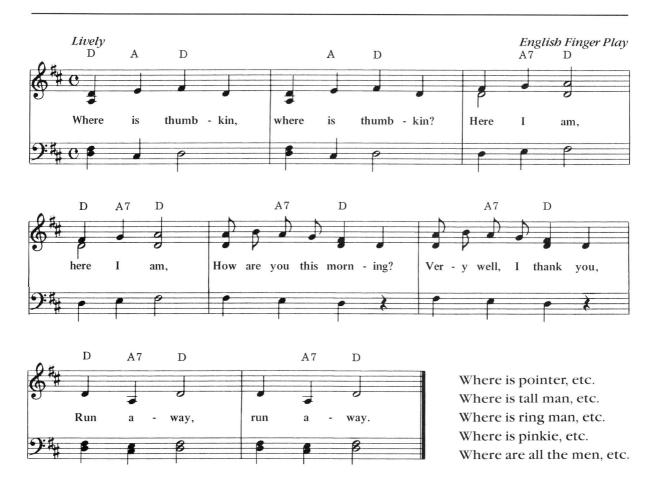

Lively   English Finger Play

Where is thumb - kin, where is thumb - kin? Here I am,

here I am, How are you this morn - ing? Ver - y well, I thank you,

Run a - way, run a - way.

Where is pointer, etc.
Where is tall man, etc.
Where is ring man, etc.
Where is pinkie, etc.
Where are all the men, etc.

Put your hands behind your back. On "Here I am," bring out the right hand, closed, with the thumb up; then the left hand, closed, with the thumb up. On "How are you this morning?" right thumb wiggles; on "Very well, I thank you," left thumb wiggles. On "Run away," put right hand behind back, then left hand behind back.

Follow the same procedure for all the other fingers. On "Where are all the men?" the whole hand comes out, wiggling fingers and making hand movements as you sing "How are you this morning?" and "Very well, we thank you." On "Run away, run away," the hands return behind the back.

Children learn this at once, and enjoy doing it with their friends.

Sing a Song of Sixpence

Scholars have advanced many explanations for the references in this song. It may even include a reference to the first English printed Bible. Today, children are fascinated by the unexpected twists the words take-especially the ending!

Briskly   English Traditional Song

Sing a song of six - pence, a pock - et full of rye,

Four - and - twen - ty black - birds baked in a pie;

When the pie was o - pened, the birds be - gan to sing,

Was - n't that a dain - ty dish to set be - fore the King?

The King was in his counting house, counting out his money,
The Queen was in the parlor, eating bread and honey,
The maid was in the garden, hanging out the clothes,
Along came a blackbird and nipped off her nose!

Pop! Goes the Weasel

Brightly

English Traditional Song

All a-round the cob-bler's bench, The mon-key chased the wea-sel; The mon-key thought 'twas all ___ in fun, Pop! goes the wea-sel.

I've no time to sit ___ and sigh, No pa-tience to wait till time ___ goes by;

Kiss me quick, I'm off, good-bye, Pop! goes the wea-sel.

The North Wind Doth Blow

English Traditional Song
Arranged by J. Hart

With expression

Em

The north wind doth blow, And we shall have

Em   Am   Em+6   Am+6

snow, And what will the rob - in do then, poor thing? He'll

G7   Edim   F#m   D7♭5

sit in the barn, and keep him - self warm, And

Em+6   C7   Em   Am   Em

hide his head un - der his wing, poor thing!

33

The Muffin Man

English Traditional Song

Smoothly

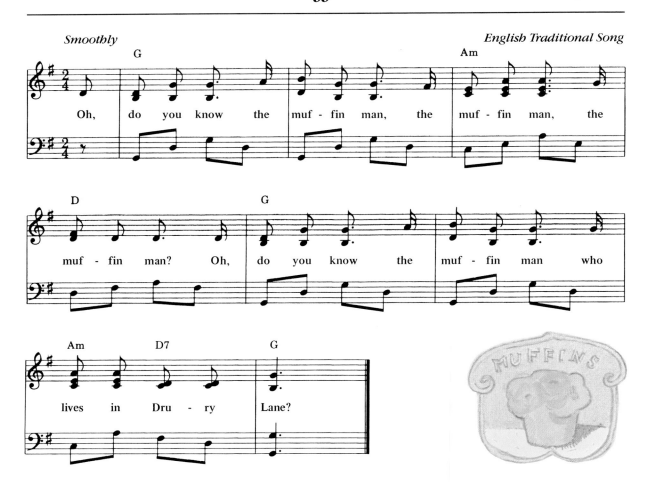

Oh, do you know the muf-fin man, the muf-fin man, the muf-fin man? Oh, do you know the muf-fin man who lives in Dru-ry Lane?

Oh, yes, we know the muffin man, the muffin man, the muffin man,
Oh, yes, we know the muffin man who lives in Drury Lane.

Little Tommy Tucker

Wandering performers sang for their suppers at English inns and taverns. They were the originators of many nursery rhymes.

Whimsically

English Traditional Song

Lit - tle Tom - my Tuck - er Sings ___ for his sup - per,

What shall he sing for? White bread and but - ter. How shall he cut it with -

out an - y knife? How shall he mar - ry ___ with - out an - y wife?

Little Jack Horner

Simply

English Traditional Song

F   B♭   Gm   C7

Lit - tle Jack Hor - ner   sat in a cor - ner,   Eat - ing his Christ - mas

F   A7   B♭   G7

pie; _____ He   put in his thumb, and   pulled out a plum, And

C   C7   F

said,   "What a   good boy am   I!" _____

See-Saw, Marjorie Daw

Briskly

English Traditional Song

See - saw, Mar - jor - ie Daw, Jack shall have a new mas - ter; He shall have but a pen - ny a day, Be - cause he won't work an - y fas - ter.

Mistress Mary

Mistress Mary may have been Mary, Queen of Scots. The "pretty maids"
would have been her ladies-in-waiting.

Cheerily

English Traditional Song

Mis - tress Ma - ry, quite con - tra - ry, how does your gar - den grow? With

sil - ver bells and cock - le shells, and pret - ty maids all in a row.

Jack and Jill

English Traditional Song

Briskly

Jack and Jill went up the hill, To get a pail of wa - ter;

Jack fell down and broke his crown, And Jill came tum - bling af - ter.

Little Miss Muffet

It is likely that this song had political origins, like so many old English nursery favorites, but the references are obscure now. That children still enjoy the song is indisputable.

Doctor Foster

Gloucester is pronounced "Gloss-ter." The song is thought to refer to a
visit by Edward the First to that city, during which his horse sank so
deeply into mud that planks had to be laid to enable the royal rider
to get out. King Edward was not pleased.

English Nursery Rhyme
Pompously

L. Hart

Doc - tor Fos - ter went to Glou - cester In a show - er of

rain, He stepped in a pud - dle right up to his mid - dle, And

nev - er went there a - gain.

There Was an Old Woman

English Traditional Song

Gaily

There was an old wom-an tossed up in a bas-ket Sev-en-teen
times as high as the moon. And where was she go-ing, I
could-n't but ask it, For in her hand she car-ried a broom. "Old

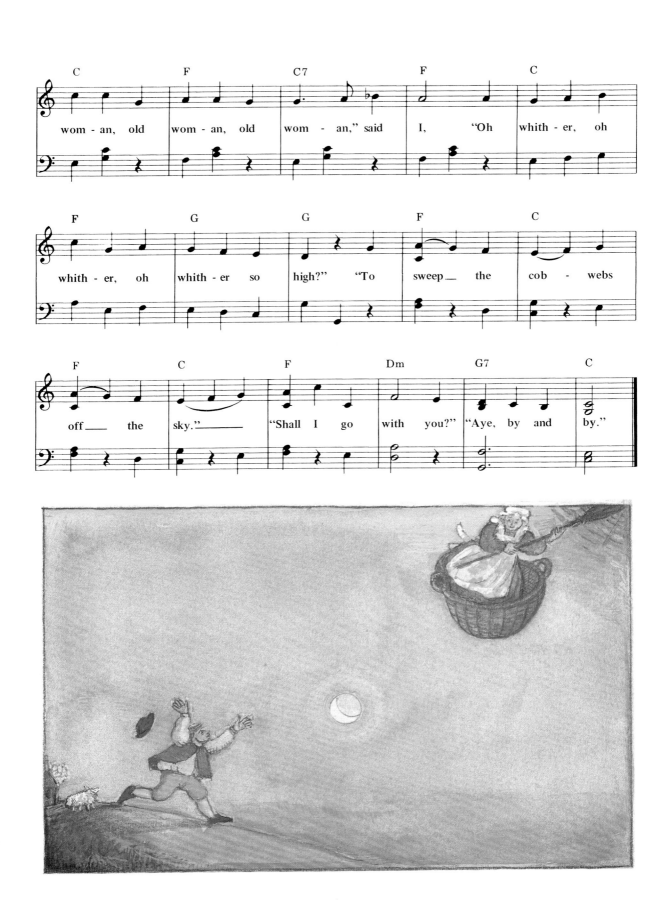

woman, old woman, old woman," said I, "Oh whither, oh whither, oh whither so high?" "To sweep the cobwebs off the sky." "Shall I go with you?" "Aye, by and by."

Over in the Meadow

Smoothly

English Traditional Song

O-ver in the mead-ow, in the sand, in the sun, Lived an old ___ moth-er frog ___ and her lit-tle frog-gie one. "Croak!" said the moth-er; "I croak," said the one, So they croaked and they croaked in the sand, in the sun.

Over in the meadow, in the stream so blue,
Lived an old mother fish and her little fishies two.
"Swim!" said the mother; "We swim," said the two,
So they swam and they swam in the stream so blue.

Over in the meadow, on a branch of the tree,
Lived an old mother bird and her little birdies three.
"Sing!" said the mother; "We sing," said the three,
So they sang and they sang on a branch of the tree.

Rub-a-Dub-Dub

Rollicking

English Traditional Song

Rub - a - dub - dub, three men in a tub, And who do you think they be?_____ The butch - er, the bak - er, the can - dle - stick mak - er,

Run them down, run them down, Rogues! All three.

I Love Little Pussy

Tenderly

English Traditional Song

I — love lit - tle puss - y, her coat is so warm, — And — if I don't hurt her, she'll do me no harm; — I'll — sit by the fire and give her some food, And — puss - y will love me be - cause I am good.

Baa, Baa, Black Sheep

This song probably originated as a protest against the amount of wool that went to the king and the rich nobility. The rhyme has changed little in two hundred years.

Lightly

English Traditional Song

Baa, baa, black sheep, have you an-y wool? Yes, sir, yes, sir,

three bags full; One for my mas - ter, one for my dame, But

none for the lit - tle boy who lives in the lane.

47

Simple Simon

English Traditional Song

With a steady beat

Simple Simon met a pieman Going to the fair. Said

Simple Simon to the pieman, "Let me taste your ware."

Said the man to Simple Simon, "Show me first your pen-ny." Said

Simple Simon to the pieman, "Indeed, I have not any."_____

Rain, Rain

Universal Folk Melody

C

Rain, rain, go a - way, Come a - gain an - oth - er day;

G7   C

Rain, rain, go a - way, Lit - tle John - ny wants to play.

Pianists – try this or improvise your own variation:

Rain, rain, go a - way, Come a - gain an - oth - er day;

Rain, rain, go a - way, Lit - tle John - ny wants to play.

Pussy Cat, Pussy Cat

English Traditional Song

Smoothly

Pus - sy cat, pus - sy cat, where have you been? I've been to Lon - don to vis - it the Queen. Pus - sy cat, pus - sy cat, what did you there? I fright - ened a lit - tle mouse un - der her chair.

Hickory Dickory Dock

Back to the days of grandfather clocks! One of the oldest limericks.

With a steady beat

English Traditional Song

Hick - o - ry dick - o - ry dock, The mouse ran up the

clock. The clock struck one, ___ The mouse ran down,

Hick - o - ry dick - o - ry dock. ___

Ride a Cock Horse

With spirit

English Traditional Song

Ride a cock horse to Ban - bur - y Cross, To

see a fine la - dy up - on a white horse;

Rings on her fin - gers and bells on her toes,

She shall have mu - sic where ev - er she goes.

Little Nut Tree

Lightly

English Traditional Song

I had a lit-tle nut tree, noth-ing would it bear,

But a sil-ver nut-meg and a gold-en pear. The

King of Spain's daugh-ter came to vis-it me, And

all for the sake of my lit-tle nut tree.

Hark, Hark!

English Traditional Song

Briskly

G   Em   D   G   D   G

Hark, hark! The dogs do bark, Beg-gars are com-ing to town;____

G   C   G   D   G

Some in rags, some in tags, And some__ in vel - vet gowns.____

54

Hippity Hop to the Barber Shop

Gaily   *English Traditional Song*

Hip - pi - ty hop to the bar - ber shop, To buy a stick of can - dy.

One for you and one for me, And one for sis - ter An - nie.

Tom, Tom, the Piper's Son

English Traditional Song
Adapted by J. Hart

With a lilt

Tom, Tom, the pip-er's son, he learned to play__ when__ he was young; And all the tune__ that__ he could play was "O-ver the hills__ and__ far a-way." Tom with his pipe__ made such a noise, that he pleased both girls and boys; and they stopped to hear him play, "O-ver the hills__ and__ far a-way."

Goosey, Goosey, Gander

The event this song refers to has long since been forgotten, but the surprise in the last line keeps it endlessly popular with children.

English Traditional Song

Goo - sey, goo - sey, gan - der, whith - er do you wan - der?

Up - stairs, down - stairs, in my la - dy's cham - ber.

There I met an old man who would not say his prayers; I

took him by the left leg and threw him down the stairs.

Mary Had a Little Lamb

*This famous English folk song was first published in America in 1830.
In 1857 it appeared in* McGuffey's Second Reader, *for fifty years a
standard textbook in America's public schools.*

Cheerily   *English Traditional Song*

Ma – ry had a   lit – tle lamb,   lit – tle lamb,   lit – tle lamb,

Ma – ry had a   lit – tle lamb, its   fleece was white as   snow.

It followed her to school one day,
school one day, school one day,
It followed her to school one day,
which was against the rule.

It made the children laugh and play,
laugh and play, laugh and play,
It made the children laugh and play
to see a lamb at school.

And so the teacher turned it out,
turned it out, turned it out,
And so the teacher turned it out,
but still it lingered near.

What makes the lamb love Mary so?
Mary so, Mary so,
What makes the lamb love Mary so?
the eager children cry.

Why, Mary loves the lamb, you know,
lamb, you know, lamb, you know,
Why, Mary loves the lamb, you know,
the teacher did reply.

Merrily We Roll Along

(To the same music as *Mary Had a Little Lamb*)

Mer-ri-ly we roll a-long, roll a-long, roll a-long,
Mer-ri-ly we roll a-long, o'er the deep blue sea.

Polly, Put the Kettle On

English Traditional Song

Curly Locks

Scottish version of this old song begins with "Bonnie lass, bonnie lass."

English Folk Song

Tenderly

Cur - ly locks, cur - ly locks, Will you be mine? You
shall not wash dish - es Nor yet feed the swine, But
sit on a cush - ion and sew a fine seam; And
feed up - on straw - ber - ries, su - gar and cream.

Lazy Mary

English Traditional Song

Firmly

La - zy Ma - ry, will you get up, Will you get up, will you get up?

La - zy Ma - ry, will you get up, Will you get up to - day?

No, no, Mother, I won't get up,
I won't get up, I won't get up;
No, no, Mother, I won't get up,
I won't get up today!

Little Drops of Water

English Traditional Song

Lightly

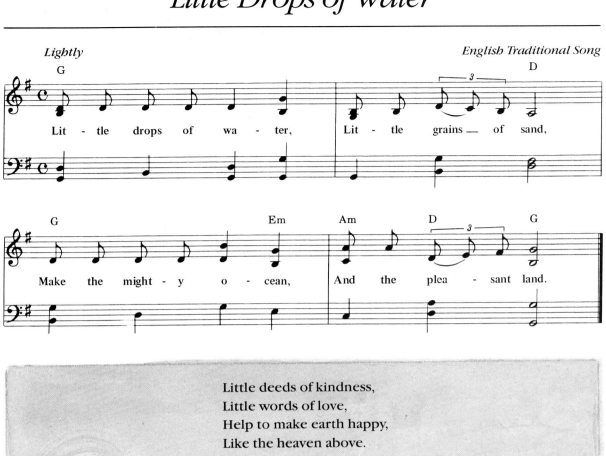

Lit - tle drops of wa - ter, Lit - tle grains — of sand,

Make the might - y o - cean, And the plea - sant land.

Little deeds of kindness,
Little words of love,
Help to make earth happy,
Like the heaven above.

Twinkle, Twinkle, Little Star

With spirit

English Traditional Song

Twin - kle, twin - kle, lit - tle star, How I won - der what you are,

Up a - bove the world so high, Like a dia - mond in the sky.

Twin - kle, twin - kle, lit - tle star, How I won - der what you are!

When the blazing sun is gone,
When he nothing shines upon,
Then you show your little light,
Twinkle, twinkle all the night.
Twinkle, twinkle little star,
How I wonder what you are!

Then the traveler in the dark
Thanks you for your tiny spark;
He could not see which way to go,
If you did not twinkle so.
Twinkle, twinkle, little star,
How I wonder what you are!

Little Bo-Peep

English Traditional Song

Lit-tle Bo-Peep has lost her sheep, And can't tell where_ to find them;

Leave them a-lone, and they'll come home, Wag-ging their tails_ be-hind them.

Little Bo-Peep fell fast asleep
And dreamed she heard them bleating;
But when she woke, 'twas all a joke.
For they were still a-fleeting.

Then up she took her little crook,
And vowed that she would find them;
What was her joy to see them there,
Wagging their tails behind them.

Lavender's Blue

English Traditional Song

Lightly

Lav - en - der's blue, dil - ly, dil - ly, lav - en - der's green;

When I am King, dil - ly, dil - ly, you shall be Queen.

Who told you so, dil - ly, dil - ly, who told you so?

'Twas my own heart, dil - ly, dil - ly, that told me so.

Hey Diddle Diddle

Probably the best-known nonsense verse in the English language. It may originally have referred to Queen Elizabeth the First, who was fond of dancing in her chambers with members of her court.

Brightly

English Traditional Song

Hey did - dle did - dle, The cat and the fid - dle, The cow jumped o - ver the moon, ___ The lit - tle dog laughed ___ to see such sport, And the dish ran a - way with the spoon. ___

Cock-a-Doodle-Doo!

Brightly

English Traditional Song

Cock - a - doo - dle - doo! My dame has lost her shoe; My mas - ter's lost his fid - dling stick, And does - n't know what to do.

Cock-a-doodle-doo!
What is my dame to do?
Till master finds his fiddling stick
She'll dance without her shoe.

68

John Peel

"Ken" is an old word for "know."

With a lilt

English Hunting Song

Do ye ken John Peel with his coat so gay, Do ye
ken John Peel at the break of day, Do ye ken John Peel when he's
far, far a-way, With his hounds and his horn in the morn-ing?

Little Boy Blue

English Traditional Song

Lightly

Lit - tle Boy Blue, come blow —— your horn, The sheep's in the mead - ow, the cow's in the corn. Where is the boy who looks af - ter the sheep? He's un - der the hay - stack, fast a - sleep.

Humpty Dumpty

Lively

English Traditional Song

D | A7 | D
Hump - ty Dump - ty sat on a wall, Hump - ty Dump - ty

A7 | D | G | D | Em | D
had a great fall; All the King's hors - es and all the King's men

A7 | D | G | A7 | D
Could - n't put Hump - ty to - geth - er a - gain.

Three Little Kittens

Brightly

English Traditional Song

Three lit - tle kit - tens, they lost their mit - tens, And they be - gan to cry:_____ "Oh, moth - er dear, see here, see here, Our mit - tens we have lost!"_____ "What, lost your mit - tens? You naugh - ty kit - tens! Then you shall have no pie."_____ "Me - ow!_____ Me - ow!_____ Me - ow!_____ Me - ow!"

Three little kittens, they found their mittens,
And they began to cry:
"Oh, Mother dear, see here, see here,
Our mittens we have found!"
"What, found your mittens? You darling kittens!
Then you shall have some pie."
"Meow! Meow! Meow! Meow!"

Three little kittens put on their mittens
And soon ate up the pie.
"Oh, Mother dear, we greatly fear,
Our mittens we have soiled."
"What, soiled your mittens? You naughty kittens!"
And they began to sigh,
"Meow! Meow! Meow! Meow!"

Three little kittens, they washed their mittens,
And hung them up to dry.
"Oh, Mother dear, see here, see here,
Our mittens we have washed."
"What, washed your mittens? You darling kittens!
But I smell a mouse close by!
Hush! Hush! Hush! Hush!"

Old King Cole

Rollicking

English Traditional Song

Em   Em+7   Gmaj7   Em+6

Old King Cole was a mer - ry old ___ soul, And a

C7   Am7   Em   F#dim

mer - ry old soul was he;   He ___ called for his pipe, and he

G7   F#7   Em   B7   Em

called for his bowl, And he called for his fid - dlers ___ three.

Ev - 'ry___ fid - dler ___ had ___ a ___ fid - dle, and a

ve - ry fine ___ fid - dle had ___ he; ___ Twee - dle dee, twee - dle dee, Went the

fid - dlers ___ three, And ___ mer - ry we ___ will ___ be.

Diddle, Diddle, Dumpling

*"Diddle, diddle, dumpling" probably was the street cry of
hot-dumpling sellers.*

Playfully   *English Traditional Song*

Did - dle, did - dle, dump - ling, my son John, Went to bed with his

trous - ers on, One stock - ing off and one stock - ing on.

Did - dle, did - dle, dump - ling, my son John.

Five Little Chickadees

Lightly

American Singing Game

Verse: Four little chickadees sitting on a tree,
One flew away and then there were three;
Chorus
Verse: Three little chickadees looking at you,
One flew away and then there were two;
Chorus
Verse: Two little chickadees sitting in the sun,
One flew away and then there was one;
Chorus
Verse: One little chickadee left all alone,
It flew away and then there were none;
Chorus

This can be a game with children acting out the verses and "flying" across the room, or it can be a finger play, with each finger representing a chickadee.

The Farmer in the Dell

English Traditional Singing Game

The farmer takes a wife, etc.
The wife takes a child, etc.
The child takes a nurse, etc.
The nurse takes a dog, etc.
The dog takes a cat, etc.
The cat takes a rat, etc.
The rat takes the cheese, etc.
The cheese stands alone, etc.

Children form a circle with one child as "farmer" in the middle. They join hands and sing while dancing around the farmer. He chooses a wife to join him, etc. On the last verse the child chosen to be the cheese stands alone, and becomes the farmer for the next game.

The Mulberry Bush

With gusto

English Traditional Singing Game

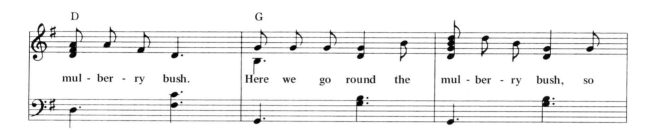

Here we go round the mul-ber-ry bush, the mul-ber-ry bush, the mul-ber-ry bush. Here we go round the mul-ber-ry bush, so ear-ly in the morn-ing.

This is the way we wash our clothes, etc.,
So early Monday morning.

This is the way we iron our clothes, etc.,
So early Tuesday morning.

This is the way we mend our clothes, etc.,
So early Wednesday morning.

This is the way we scrub the floor, etc.,
So early Thursday morning.

This is the way we sweep the house, etc.,
So early Friday morning.

This is the way we bake our bread, etc.,
So early Saturday morning.

This is the way we go to church, etc.,
So early Sunday morning.

Nuts in May

(To the same music as The Mulberry Bush)

1. Here we come gath'ring nuts in May,
   nuts in May, nuts in May,
   Here we come gath'ring nuts in May,
   all on a frosty morning.

2. Whom will you have for nuts in May,
   nuts in May, nuts in May,
   Whom will you have for nuts in May,
   all on a frosty morning?

3. We will have Mary for nuts in May,
   nuts in May, nuts in May,
   We will have Mary for nuts in May,
   all on a frosty morning.

4. Whom will you send to fetch her away,
   fetch her away, fetch her away,
   Whom will you send to fetch her away,
   all on a frosty morning?

5. We will send Betty to fetch her away,
   fetch her away, fetch her away,
   We will send Betty to fetch her away,
   all on a frosty morning.

Children form two lines, holding hands; they advance toward each other, then fall back. One line sings verses 1, 3, 5, and the other sings 2, 4 in reply. The leader, at the end of the first line, fetches a child in the opposite line, on cue, and both return. When all but one are in the first line, the child who is left becomes leader and brings the others back to that side. Children's actual names are used.

Bingo

American Folk Song

Sing through once. Then, singing faster each time through, clap once instead of singing "B," twice instead of singing "B-I," and so forth.

Bluebird

Take a little girl, tap her on the shoulder,
Take a little girl, tap her on the shoulder,
Take a little girl, tap her on the shoulder,
Oh, Johnny, I am tired.

Children make a circle, hands raised to form arches. A child chosen to be a bluebird skips in and out the arches until verse two, when she chooses a second bluebird by tapping someone in the circle on the shoulder. Repeat with two bluebirds, then four, etc., until everyone is a bluebird. All fall down to rest at the words "I am tired."

The Gallant Ship

English Traditional Singing Game

Children join hands in a circle. They all take sliding steps to the left, until "and she sank" when they jump in place; jumping and crouching on "to the bottom," and jumping again on "of the sea," coming to a sitting-on-heels position and trying not to fall over.

Go Round and Round the Village

Briskly

English Traditional Singing Game

Go round and round the vil-lage, Go round and round the
vil-lage, Go round and round the vil-lage, As
we have done be-fore.

Go in and out the window,
Go in and out the window,
Go in and out the window,
As we have done before.

Stand and face your partner,
Stand and face your partner,
Stand and face your partner,
As we have done before.

Follow me to London,
Follow me to London,
Follow me to London,
As we have done before.

Now shake his hand and leave him,
Now shake his hand and leave him,
Now shake his hand and leave him,
As we have done before.

Children stand in a circle, pretending to be houses in a village. One child is IT and runs around the village during the first verse. On the second verse, those in the circle raise their arms to make windows, and IT runs in and out. On the third verse, IT chooses a partner and they both bow. On the fourth verse, partners join hands and skip around the circle. They go back inside the circle on the fifth verse, shake hands, bow; and the second child becomes IT.

Clap Your Hands

With spirit

American Folk Song

Clap, clap, clap your hands, Clap your hands to - geth - er;

Clap, clap, clap your hands, Clap your hands to - geth - er.

La la la la la la la, La la la la la la,

La la la la la la la, Clap your hands to - geth - er!

Clap your hands to - geth - er!

mf *crescendo* *ff*

Sally, Go Round

Playfully

English Traditional Singing Game

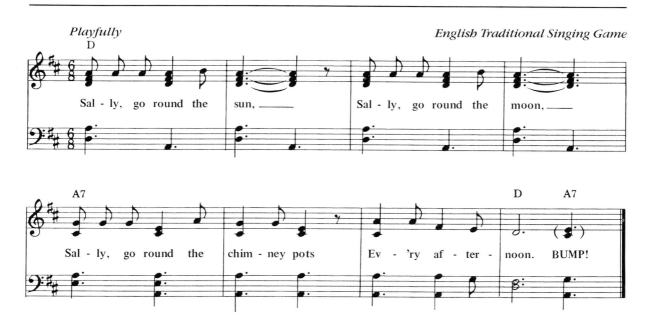

Sal - ly, go round the sun, _____ Sal - ly, go round the moon, _____

Sal - ly, go round the chim - ney pots Ev - 'ry af - ter - noon. BUMP!

Children join hands in a circle and skip around to the left; at the word "bump" they reverse and skip around to the right.

The Noble Duke of York

March time

English Traditional Singing Game

G   Am

Oh, the no-ble Duke of York, He had ten thou-sand men; He

D   D7   G

marched them up to the top of the hill, And marched them down a - gain.

Oh, when you're up you're up,
And when you're down you're down,
And when you're only halfway up,
You're neither up nor down.

Children form two lines, partners facing each other. While all are singing the first verse, the head couple marches to the foot of the set and back. On the second verse they join hands and swing around to the foot of the set again. The second couple now becomes the head couple.

A-Hunting We Will Go

(To the same music as *The Noble Duke of York*)

Oh, a-hunt-ing we will go,
A-hunt-ing we will go,
We'll catch a fox and put him in a box,
And then we'll let him go.

Oats, Peas, Beans

English Traditional Singing Game

With gusto

Oats, peas, beans, and bar-ley grow, Oats, peas, beans, and bar-ley grow, Do you or I or an-y-one know How oats, peas, beans, and bar-ley grow?

First the farmer sows his seeds,
Then he stands and takes his ease,
Stamps his feet, and claps his hand,
And turns around to view the land.

Waiting for a partner,
Waiting for a partner,
Open the ring and take one in,
And then we'll dance and gaily sing.

On the first verse, children form a circle, join hands, skip around to the left.
One child stands in the center, as the farmer.

He acts out the words of the second verse, sowing seed, turning around, and
shading his eyes to view the land.

On the third verse, he chooses a partner; all join hands and skip around
outside the farmer and his partner.

Another child becomes the farmer when the song begins again.

Skip to My Lou

American Play Party Game

Gaily

Chorus

Skip, skip, skip to my Lou, Skip, skip, skip to my Lou,

Skip, skip, skip to my Lou, Skip to my Lou, my dar - ling!

Verse

Lost my part - ner, what - 'll I do? Lost my part - ner, what - 'll I do?

F **Gm** **F** **C7** **F**

Lost my part-ner, what-'ll I do? Skip to my Lou, my dar - ling!

Chorus

Verse: I'll find another one, prettier, too,
I'll find another one, prettier, too,
I'll find another one, prettier, too,
Skip to my Lou, my darling!

Chorus

Verse: Can't get a red bird, blue bird'll do,
Can't get a red bird, blue bird'll do,
Can't get a red bird, blue bird'll do,
Skip to my Lou, my darling!

Chorus

Verse: Flies in the sugar bowl, shoo, shoo, shoo,
Flies in the sugar bowl, shoo, shoo, shoo,
Flies in the sugar bowl, shoo, shoo, shoo,
Skip to my Lou, my darling!

Children stand with partners in a circle; an extra child is in the center. All sing and clap to the chorus. On "Lost my partner," the child in the center chooses one in the circle, and in skating formation (crossed hands) they skip around the outside of the circle, the others clapping.

All skip around to the left on the chorus.

The child whose partner was taken sings "I'll get another one," chooses another, and takes his turn around the circle.

This sequence continues until the end of the dance.

Looby Loo

English Traditional Singing Game

Joyfully

Chorus F

Here we go loo-by loo,____ Here we go loo-by light,____

F / C7 / F **Verse**

Here we go loo-by loo,____ All on a Sat-ur-day night.____ I

F

put my right hand in,____ I put my right hand out,____ I

F C7 F Dm F C7 F

give my right hand a shake, shake, shake, And turn my-self a - bout.

Chorus
Verse: I put my left hand in, etc.
Chorus
Verse: I put my right foot in, etc.

Chorus
Verse: I put my left foot in, etc.
Chorus
Verse: I put my whole self in, etc.

On the chorus, children join hands in a circle and skip to the center and back, then follow the directions as they sing them.

Gogo

English version by Margaret Marks

Singing Game from Kenya

As sung by Mary Okari
Arranged by J. Hart

Children may want to organize their own Halloween parade. *Gogo* is a good song to sing as the children, wearing masks, walk in "funny ways" as they "hump and clump about."

Rig-a-Jig-Jig

Joyfully

American Play Party Game

As I was walk-ing down the street, down the street, down the street, A pret-ty {girl/boy} I chanced to meet, Heigh-ho, heigh-ho, __ heigh-ho! __ Rig-a-jig-jig and a-way we go, a-way we go, a-way we go; Rig-a-jig-jig and a-way we go, Heigh-ho, heigh-ho, __ heigh-ho! __

 Children form two circles, one inside the other. On the verse one walks around clockwise, the other counterclockwise, both singing. On the last "Heigh-ho" before the chorus they stop, face the nearest child in the other circle, take hands, and skip around during the chorus. Then they drop hands and continue the game.

I'm a Little Teapot

Give the following directions for acting out the words:

"Left hand on your hip for the handle, right hand on your shoulder for the spout, don't lean too far over to pour out!"

Did You Ever See a Lassie?

Gaily

English Traditional Singing Game

Did you ev - er see a lass - ie, a lass - ie, a lass - ie, Did you ev - er see a lass - ie go this way and that? Go this way and that way, And this way and that way, Did you ev - er see a lass - ie Go this way and that?

Children form a circle with one player in the center as IT. They skip to the left until "this way and that," when the child who is IT originates a rhythmic pattern such as clapping, stamping, swaying, which the others imitate. The center child chooses another IT and the game continues. (If a boy is IT the word "laddie" is used.)

Three White Gulls

English words by Marguerite Wilkinson

Italian Folk Song

There are three ____ white gulls ____ a - fly - ing, There are three ____ white gulls ____ a - fly - ing, There are three ____ white gulls a - fly - ing By the sea they cry, by the sea they cry, by the sea they cry.

In the sea they dip their soft wings,
In the sea they dip their soft wings,
In the sea they dip their soft wings—
Then soar to the sky, then soar to the sky,
Then soar to the sky.

When children have learned this song, they will enjoy moving around the room. The rise and fall of the melody suggests the movement of the gulls' wings.

See the Pony Galloping, Galloping

With spirit

American Folk Song

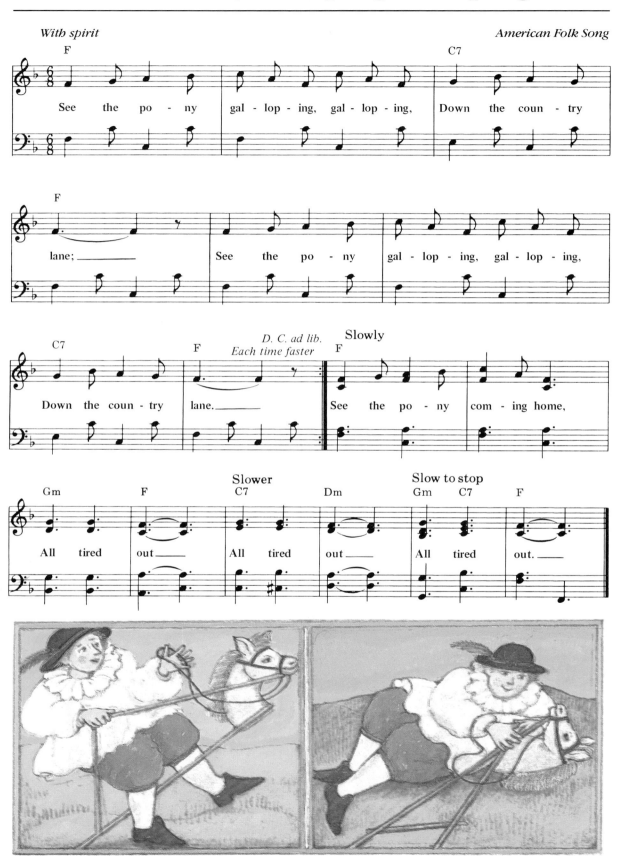

See the po - ny gal - lop - ing, gal - lop - ing, Down the coun - try lane; _____ See the po - ny gal - lop - ing, gal - lop - ing, Down the coun - try lane. _____

D. C. ad lib.
Each time faster

Slowly See the po - ny com - ing home,

Slower **Slow to stop** All tired out _____ All tired out _____ All tired out.

To Market, to Market

English Traditional Singing Game

With spirit

To mar - ket, to mar - ket, to buy a fat pig;

Home a - gain, home a - gain, jig - get - ty jig. To

mar - ket, to mar - ket, to buy a fat hog;

Home a - gain, home a - gain, jig - get - ty jog.

To market, to market, to buy a plum cake;
Home again, home again, market is late.
To market, to market, to buy a plum bun;
Home again, home again, market is done.

A Tisket, a Tasket

Brightly

Traditional Singing Game

A tis - ket, a tas - ket, a green and yel - low bas - ket; I wrote a let - ter to my love and on the way I lost it; I lost it, I lost it, and on the way I lost it; A lit - tle {boy/girl} picked it up and put it in {his/her} pock - et.

Children join hands in a circle; one child chosen to be IT holds a hand-kerchief. While all are singing, IT skips around the outside of the circle. On the last "I lost it," IT drops the handkerchief behind the nearest child. In the same direction he or she has been going, IT races around the circle; the child behind whom the handkerchief has been dropped races around the circle in the opposite direction; the last one to get back to the handkerchief is now IT and the game begins again.

Little Sally Waters

English Traditional Singing Game

Playfully

Lit – tle Sal – ly Wa – ters, sit – ting in the sun,
Cry – ing and weep – ing, ___ lone-some lit – tle one. Rise, Sal – ly, rise;
wipe off your eyes; Fly to the East, Sal – ly, Fly to the West, Sal – ly,
Fly to the one you love the ve – ry best.

The first Sally sits in the center of the circle and acts out the words as the other children sing. On cue, she rises, "flies to the East" and "flies to the West." The player she goes to on the last line becomes the next Sally, and the game goes on until all have had a turn. Children love to act this out, pretending to weep and then to fly.

Bow Belinda

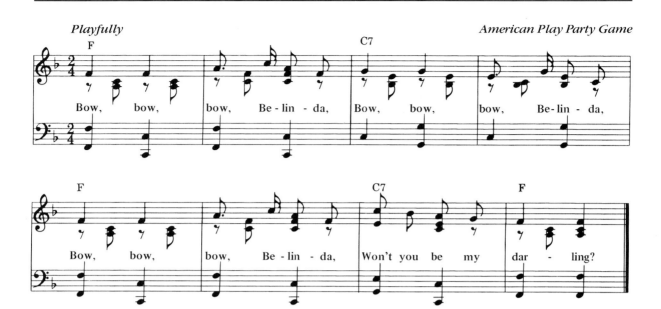

Bow, bow, bow, Be-lin-da, Bow, bow, bow, Be-lin-da,

Bow, bow, bow, Be-lin-da, Won't you be my dar-ling?

Right hand up, Oh, Belinda,
Right hand up, Oh, Belinda,
Right hand up, Oh, Belinda,
Won't you be my darling?

Left hand up, Oh, Belinda,
Left hand up, Oh, Belinda,
Left hand up, Oh, Belinda,
Won't you be my darling?

Both hands up, Oh, Belinda,
Both hands up, Oh, Belinda,
Both hands up, Oh, Belinda,
Won't you be my darling?

Shake that big foot shy all around her,
Shake that big foot shy all around her,
Shake that big foot shy all around her,
Won't you be my darling?

Promenade all, Oh, Belinda,
Promenade all, Oh, Belinda,
Promenade all, Oh, Belinda,
Won't you be my darling?

Boys line up in a row, facing equal number of girls in a row, a few feet apart.

On "Bow, bow, bow, Belinda," boys bow, girls bow or curtsy to facing partners.

On "Right hand up," partners advance, take named hand, turn around each other and back to places. This is repeated for left hand and both hands as sung.

On "Shake that big foot," all fold hands across chest, pass around partners back to back (do-si-do), and return to places.

On "Promenade all," head couple make arch with arms. Last couple take hands, march up between rows, under arch, separate, and return down outside. Remaining couples follow as soon as possible. Head couple separate and follow to become new bottom couple.

Five-year-olds love and can do this "longways" dance.

Jack, Be Nimble

For centuries, jumping over a candle has been a sport and a way of telling fortunes in England.

Briskly

English Traditional Singing Game

Jack, be nim - ble, Jack, be quick, Jack, jump o - ver the can - dle stick.

Pease Porridge Hot

This is an English clapping game, played by children on cold days to keep their hands warm.

Briskly

English Traditional Singing Game

Pease por - ridge hot, Pease por - ridge cold,

Pease por - ridge in the pot, Nine days old.

Some like it hot,
Some like it cold,
Some like it in the pot,
Nine days old.

London Bridge

Some scholars claim that this song stems from actual destruction of the bridge in the eleventh century by invading Norsemen.

Build it up with iron bars, etc.
Iron bars will bend and break, etc.
Build it up with pins and needles, etc.
Pins and needles rust and bend, etc.
Build it up with gravel and stone, etc.
Gravel and stone will wash away, etc.

Two players form the bridge by joining hands with both arms stretched upward. The other players march under the arch in single file. On "my fair lady" the arch falls, capturing a player who is asked to choose gold or silver, and then lines up behind whichever of the arch-makers represents that metal. When all players have been caught, the two lines have a tug of war.

Here Stands a Redbird

American Singing Game

Joyfully

Here stands a red-bird, Tra - la-la - la-la Here stands a red-bird,

Tra - la-la - la-la Rice, sug-ar and tea!

One child in the center of the circle makes birdlike hopping, flying, pecking,
or turning motions which the others imitate, and then selects a new Redbird.

Ring Around a Rosy

Briskly

English Traditional Singing Game

Children join hands in a circle and skip to the left while singing. On "all fall down," be sure they let go of each other's hands and fall down as easily as possible.

Sur le Pont d'Avignon

*Every year the people of Avignon, a beautiful city in southern France,
gather on their famous bridge, built by the Romans, to dance.*

French Folk Song, Dance

Joyfully

Chorus

Sur le pont d'A - vi - gnon l'on y dan - se, l'on y dan - se;

Sur le pont d'A - vi - gnon l'on y dan - se, tout en rond.

Verse: Les mesdames font comme ci,
Et puis encore comme ça.

Sur le pont d'Avignon
l'on y danse, tout en rond.

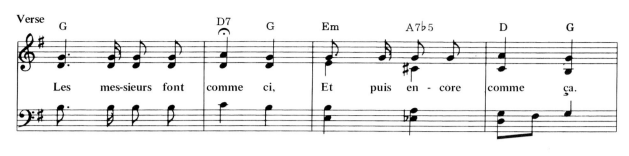

Les mes-sieurs font comme ci, Et puis en-core comme ça.

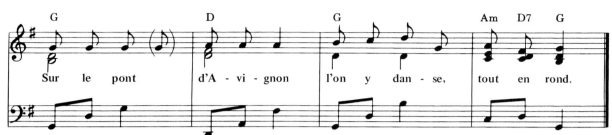

Sur le pont d'A-vi-gnon l'on y dan-se, tout en rond.

English translation

On the bridge at Avignon
They are dancing, they are dancing;
On the bridge at Avignon
They are dancing, all around.
Gentlemen go this way,
Then again go that way.
On the bridge at Avignon
They are dancing, all around.

On the bridge at Avignon
They are dancing, they are dancing;
On the bridge at Avignon
They are dancing, all around.
Ladies now go this way,
Then again go that way.
On the bridge at Avignon
They are dancing, all around.

Each boy chooses a partner; the girl stands on the right. All form a circle, join hands, and skip to the right during the chorus. On the verse, they drop hands and face each other; On "Les messieurs font comme ci," the boys bow low to one side, then to the other.

Repeat the chorus.

On the second verse, girls bow to one side, then to the other, on "Les mesdames font comme ci." Then, on "Et puis encore comme ça," girls take one step to the left and resume the dance with a new partner.

Billy Boy

Lightly

Irish-American Song

Oh, ___ where ___ have you been, Bil - ly Boy, Bil - ly Boy? Oh, ___

where have you been, charm - ing Bil - ly? I have

been to seek a wife, She's the joy ___ of my life, She's a

young thing and can - not leave her moth - er. ___

Did she ask you to come in, Billy Boy, Billy Boy?
Did she ask you to come in, charming Billy?
Yes, she asked me to come in,
There's a dimple in her chin,
She's a young thing and cannot leave her mother.

Can she make a cherry pie, Billy Boy, Billy Boy?
Can she make a cherry pie, charming Billy?
She can make a cherry pie,
Quick as a cat can wink its eye,
She's a young thing and cannot leave her mother.

How old is she, Billy Boy, Billy Boy?
How old is she, charming Billy?
Three times six and four times seven,
Twenty-eight and eleven;
She's a young thing and cannot leave her mother.

The Bear Went Over the Mountain

The amiable quality of this song's words and tune enchants children.
Its origin is unknown.

Do Your Ears Hang Low?

*A camp song from the days of the American Revolution. Children
enjoy acting it out, especially wiggling their ears.*

Humorously

American Revolutionary Folk Song

Do your ears hang low, do they wob-ble to and fro? Can you
tie them in a knot, can you tie them in a bow? Can you
fling them o - ver your shoul-der Like a Con - ti - nen - tal sol - dier, Do your
ears hang low?

Where, Oh Where Has My Little Dog Gone?

Septimus Winter
American Minstrel Song

Plaintively

Oh where, oh where has my lit - tle dog gone? Oh

where, oh where can he be?_____ With his ears cut short and his

tail cut long, Oh where, oh where_ is he?_____

Good Morning to You

"Happy Birthday" can also be sung to this melody.

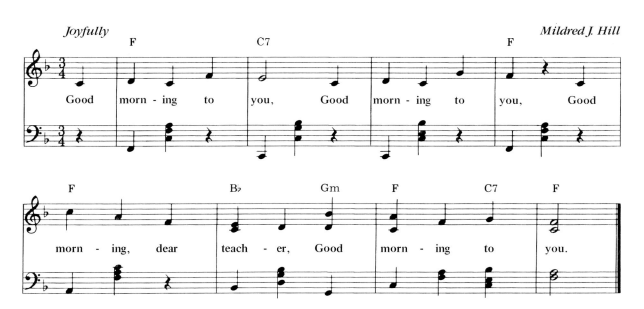

Joyfully

Mildred J. Hill

Good morn - ing to you, Good morn - ing to you, Good

morn - ing, dear teach - er, Good morn - ing to you.

Go Tell Aunt Rhody

One of the best known and loved of American folk songs, though the
goose in some regions belongs to Aunt Betty, Aunt Nancy, or names
other than Aunt Rhody. One may suspect that Auntie was not too
distressed to have her feathers at last.

With feeling

American Traditional Song

Go tell Aunt Rho - dy, Go tell Aunt Rho - dy,

Go tell Aunt Rho - dy, her old gray goose is dead. The

The one she's been saving,
The one she's been saving,
The one she's been saving,
To make a feather bed.

She died in the mill pond,
She died in the mill pond,
She died in the mill pond,
Standing on her head.

116

Street Song

A song heard in Chicago, circa 1917. Many changes can be made –
going to the grocery or bakery or any other shop, calling for your
other friends besides Willie – but make the E-I-O loud and clear, so
he'll hear you in the next block.

W. Greene
With gusto

American Folk Song

Up to the bar - ber shop I go, I can - not stay an - y long - er, For if I do my moth - er will say I played with the boys on the cor - ner. E - I - O for Wil - lie, E - I - O for Wil - lie; Won't you come, Won't you come, Won't you come and play with me?

Old MacDonald Had a Farm

Traditional English-American Song

Bouncy

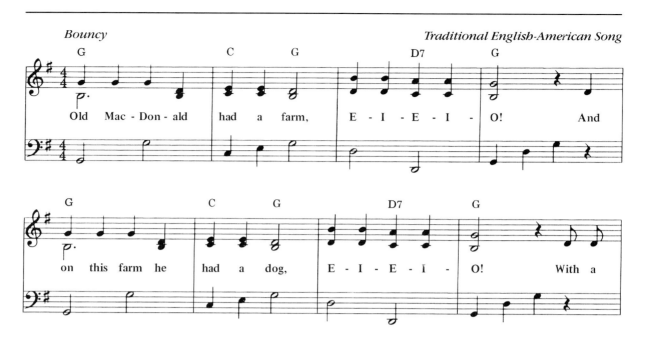

Old Mac-Don-ald had a farm, E - I - E - I - O! And

on this farm he had a dog, E - I - E - I - O! With a

And on this farm he had some ducks,
E-I-E-I-O!
With a quack, quack here, and a quack, quack there,
Here a quack, there a quack, ev'ry where a quack, quack,

With a bow-wow here, and a bow-wow there,
Here a bow, there a bow, ev'ry where a bow-wow,
Old MacDonald had a farm, E-I-E-I-O!

Continue with animals and their sounds:
Chick—chick, chick here, etc.
Cow—moo, moo here, etc.
Pig—oink, oink here, etc.
Horse—neigh, neigh here, etc.
Cat—meow, meow here, etc.

This is a cumulative song, and can be continued until all the animals of the farmyard have been named.

There's a Little Wheel A-Turning

American Spiritual

Lyrically

There's a lit-tle wheel a-turn-ing in my heart, _____ There's a
lit-tle wheel a-turn-ing in my heart. In my heart _____ In my
heart _____ There's a lit-tle wheel a-turn-ing in my heart.

There's a little song a-singing in my heart,
There's a little song a-singing in my heart.
In my heart–In my heart–
There's a little song a-singing in my heart.

Oh, I feel so very happy in my heart,
I feel so very happy in my heart.
In my heart–In my heart–
I feel so very happy in my heart.

Roll Over

Humorously

American Folk Song

Ten in the bed, and the lit-tle one said, "Roll o - ver! Roll o - ver!" They all rolled o - ver and one fell out.

Nine in the bed, etc.
Eight in the bed, etc.
Seven in the bed, etc.
Six in the bed, etc.
Five in the bed, etc.
Four in the bed, etc.
Three in the bed, etc.
Two in the bed, etc.
One in the bed, and the little one said,
"Alone at last!"

Yankee Doodle

*The famous tune was used by the British to make fun of the Americans
during the first part of the Revolution. But the Americans made
it their own in the later years of the war, and so has it been ever since.*

With martial precision   *English-American Folk Song*

Verse

Yan - kee Doo - dle went to town, a - rid - ing on a po - ny, He
stuck a feath - er in his cap and called it mac - a - ro - ni!

Chorus

Yan - kee Doo - dle, keep it up, Yan - kee Doo - dle dan - dy;

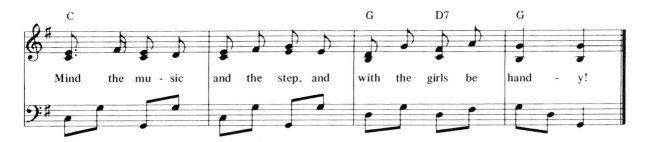

Mind the mu - sic and the step, and with the girls be hand - y!

Verse: Father and I went down to camp,
Along with Captain Gooding,
And there we saw the men and boys
As thick as hasty pudding.
Chorus

Verse: And there was Captain Washington
Upon a slapping stallion,
A-giving orders to his men,
I guess there was a million.
Chorus

Verse: And there I saw a little keg,
The head was made of leather;
They knocked on it with little sticks
To call the folks together.
Chorus

Eletelephony

Laura Elizabeth Richards
With clarity

J. Hart

Once there was an el - e - phant, Who tried to use the tel - e - phant— No! No! I mean an el - e - phone Who tried to use the the tel - e - phone (Dear me, I am not cer - tain quite That e - ven now I've got it right.)

Oh, Susanna!

*One of the best-known American songs of all time. First performed
in a minstrel show in 1848, it became popular with the forty-niners
as they headed West, and has never lost its appeal.*

Briskly

Stephen Collins Foster

Verse

D

I___ come from Al - a - bam - a with my ban - jo on my

A   D   E7

knee;   I'm___ going to Lou' - si - an - a, my___

D   A7   D

true love for to see. It ___ rained all night the day I left, The

D   A   D

weath - er it was dry; The ___ sun so hot I

froze to death, Su - san - na, don't you cry.

Chorus

Oh, Su - san - na! Oh, don't you cry for me, I___

come from Al - a - bam - a with my ban - jo on my knee.

Verse: I had a dream the other night
When everything was still;
I thought I saw Susanna come
A-walking down the hill.
The red, red rose was in her hand,
The tear was in her eye;
I said, "I come from Alabam',
Susanna, don't you cry."
Chorus

She'll Be Coming Round the Mountain

One of the earliest railroad songs of our country, this has many versions.

She'll be driving six white horses when she comes, (spoken) whoa, back, etc.

And we'll all sing "Hallelujah" when she comes, (spoken) oh, yes, etc.

Down by the Station

Today's children may never have seen a steam engine, but they enjoy puffing like locomotives and moving fists like pistons as they march around.

Briskly

American Folk Song

Down by the sta - tion, ear - ly in the morn - ing,

See the lit - tle puff - er - bil - lies all in a row;

See the en - gine dri - ver pull the lit - tle throt - tle,

Chug, Chug, Poof, Poof! Off we go!

The Bus Song

Joyfully

Adapted with new words by Tom Glazer

1. The peo-ple in the bus go up and down, Up and down, up and down. The peo-ple in the bus go up and down, All a-round the town. _____ 2. The

1. Children go up and down in their seats.
2. Hold arms out and imitate wipers by waving forearms.
3. Pull an imaginary hand-brake up three times to "roomp, roomp, roomp."
4. Tap thumb against forefinger three times (same hand) to "clink, clink, clink."
5. Describe circles with both hands to "round and round."
6. Rock arms as if holding a baby.

2. The wiper on the bus goes "Swish, swish, swish,
   Swish, swish, swish; swish, swish, swish."
   The wiper on the bus goes "Swish, swish, swish,"
   All around the town.
3. The brake on the bus goes "Roomp, roomp, roomp,
   Roomp, roomp, roomp; roomp, roomp, roomp!"
   The brake on the bus goes "Roomp, roomp, roomp,"
   All around the town.
4. The money in the bus goes "Clink, clink, clink,
   Clink, clink, clink; clink, clink, clink."
   The money in the bus goes "Clink, clink, clink,"
   All around the town.
5. The wheels on the bus go round and round,
   Round and round, round and round.
   The wheels on the bus go round and round,
   All around the town.
6. There's a baby on the bus goes "Wah, wah, wah,
   Wah, wah, wah; wah, wah, wah."
   There's a baby on the bus goes "Wah, wah, wah,"
   All around the town.

Working on the Railroad

American Traditional Song

Frère Jacques

French Traditional Round

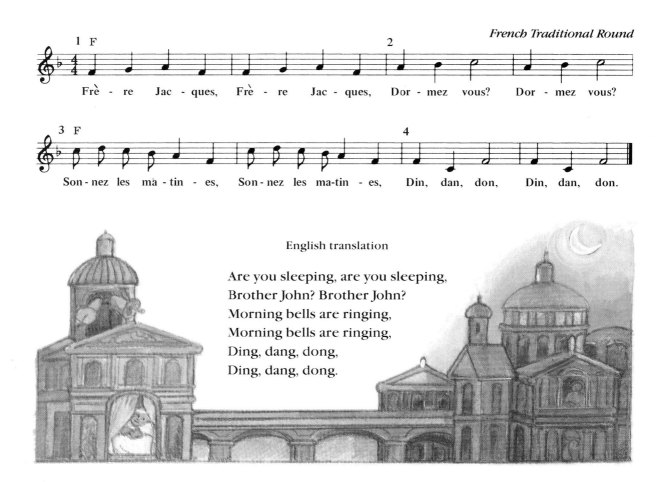

Frè - re Jac - ques, Frè - re Jac - ques, Dor - mez vous? Dor - mez vous?

Son - nez les ma - tin - es, Son - nez les ma-tin - es, Din, dan, don, Din, dan, don.

English translation

Are you sleeping, are you sleeping,
Brother John? Brother John?
Morning bells are ringing,
Morning bells are ringing,
Ding, dang, dong,
Ding, dang, dong.

Oh, How Lovely Is the Evening

English Traditional Round

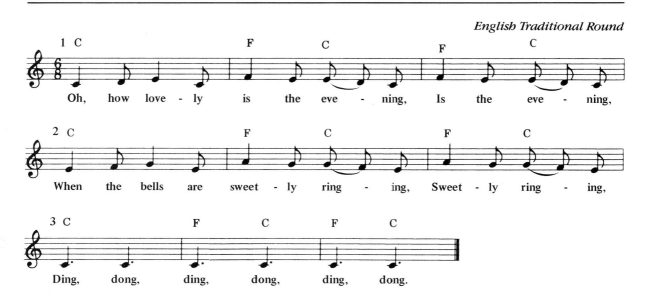

Oh, how love - ly is the eve - ning, Is the eve - ning,

When the bells are sweet - ly ring - ing, Sweet - ly ring - ing,

Ding, dong, ding, dong, ding, dong.

Row, Row, Row Your Boat

English Traditional Round

1 C · 2 C

Row, row, row your boat Gent - ly down the stream; _____

3 C

Mer - ri - ly, mer - ri - ly, mer - ri - ly, mer - ri - ly,

4 C   G   C

Life is but a dream. _____

El Coquito (The Little Tree Toad)

Puerto Rican Lullaby

Mexican Counting Song

Brightly

Mexican Folk Song

U - no, dos, y tres, cua - tro, cin - co, seis,

Sie - te, o - cho, nue - ve, I can count to diez.

La la la la la La la la la la

1.
La la la la la la!

2.
la la la!

English translation

Uno–one
Dos–two
Tres–three
Cuatro–four
Cinco–five
Seis–six
Siete–seven
Ocho–eight
Nueve–nine
Diez–ten

Lightly Row

German Folk Song

With a steady beat

Light - ly row, light - ly row, o'er the glass - y waves we go;

Smooth - ly glide, smooth - ly glide, on the si - lent tide.

Let the wind and wa - ters be min - gled with our mel - o - dy;

Sing and float, sing and float, in our lit - tle boat.

I Saw Three Ships

Joyfully

English Traditional Holiday Song

I saw three ships come sail - ing by, A - sail - ing by, a - sail - ing by; I saw three ships come sail - ing by, On New__ Year's Day in the morn - ing.

And what do you think was in them then,
Was in them then, was in them then?
And what do you think was in them then,
On New Year's Day in the morning?

Three pretty girls were in them then,
Were in them then, were in them then,
Three pretty girls were in them then,
On New Year's Day in the morning.

And one could whistle and one could sing,
And one could play the violin;
Such joy there was at my wedding,
On New Year's Day in the morning.

Hot Cross Buns

A street cry from London. Hot cross buns were traditionally eaten for breakfast on Good Friday.

With gusto

English Traditional Song

The Easter Bunny

An original song from the children in Sue Raymond's nursery school class in Westport, Connecticut.

Over the River and Through the Wood

Smoothly

American Traditional Song

O - ver the riv - er and through the wood, To grand - moth - er's house we

go; _____ The horse knows the way to car - ry the sleigh, through

white and drift - ed snow _____ O - ver the riv - er and

through the wood, Oh, how the wind does blow!_____ It stings the toes and bites the nose, As o-ver the fields we go!_____

Over the river and through the wood,
Trot fast, my dapple gray!
Spring over the ground like a hunting hound,
For this is Thanksgiving Day!
Over the river and through the wood,
Now grandmother's cap I spy!
Hurrah for the fun! Is the pudding done?
Hurrah for the pumpkin pie!

Hanukkah Song

The Hebrew word Hanukkah means dedication. During the Festival of Lights, candles are lit on eight successive nights. The menorah is the candelabrum, the hora a traditional dance.

Jewish Folk Song

Joyfully

Dm A7 Dm

Oh, Ha-nuk-kah, Oh, Ha-nuk-kah, come light the me-no-rah.

Dm A7 Dm

Let's have a par-ty, we'll all dance the ho-ra.

Dm A7 Dm

Gath-er round the ta-ble, we'll give you a treat.

Gm A7 Dm

Shin-ing tops to play with and pan-cakes to eat. And

while we _____ are danc - ing, _____ the

can - dles are burn - ing _____ low; _____

One for each night, they will shed a sweet light To re -

1.
mind us of days long a - go; _____

2.
days long a - go. _____

Santa's Chimney

My husband and I wrote this song when our children were little, and it has become a part of our Christmas tradition.

Telling a story

L. and J. Hart

Verse

We used to live in an old - fash - ioned house With an at - tic and stairs, and a fire - place this wide; And a big tall chim - in - ey up to the roof Down which San - ta Claus could slide. But now, more's the pit - y, we live in the cit - y, No at - tic, no stairs, no fi - re - place nice and wide; That's why we're wor - ry - ing, we'd

Jingle Bells

The words and music to this popular holiday song were written by
John Pierpont, a Unitarian minister who was born in 1785.

Pat-a-Pan

Burgundian Carol

Merrily

Chil - dren, bring your flute and drum, For the jol - ly time has come; We'll be mer - ry as you play, Tu - ra - lu - ra - lu, pat - a - pat - a - pan, We'll be mer - ry as you play, For a Christ - mas should be gay!

We Wish You a Merry Christmas

With gusto

English Traditional Holiday Song

Now bring us a figgy pudding,
Now bring us a figgy pudding,
Now bring us a figgy pudding,
And bring it out here.

We won't go until we get some,
We won't go until we get some,
We won't go until we get some,
So bring it out here.

We wish you a merry Christmas,
We wish you a merry Christmas,
We wish you a merry Christmas
And a happy New Year!

Title Index

Subject Index

Mothers and Fathers

Nonsense Songs

Nursery Rhymes – *see* Mother
Goose Songs

Other Lands – *see* Around the World

Playing – *see* Having Fun

Rounds

Sad Songs – *see* Feeling Bad

Songs with a Lesson

Travel – *see* Going Places

Weather

Working and Doing Chores

This book belongs to:

....

Text by Chris Hawkes
Senior Editor James Mitchem
US Editor Margaret Parrish
US Senior Editor Shannon Beatty
Senior Art Editor Victoria Palastanga
Edited by Hélène Hilton, Becky Walsh
Designed and illustrated by Jim Green, Karen Hood,
Hannah Moore, Rhys Thomas, Sadie Thomas
Design assistance Eleanor Bates
Additional illustrations Shahid Mahmood
Project Picture Researcher Sakshi Saluja
Senior Producer, Pre-Production Tony Phipps
Producer John Casey
Jacket Coordinator Issy Walsh
Creative Technical Support Sonia Charbonnier
Managing Editor Penny Smith
Managing Art Editor Mabel Chan
Publishing Director Sarah Larter
Creative Director Helen Senior

First American Edition, 2020
Published in the United States by DK Publishing
1450 Broadway, Suite 801, New York, New York 10018

A catalog record for this book is available from the Library of Congress.
ISBN 978-1-4654-9151-0

DK books are available at special discounts when purchased in bulk for
sales promotions, premiums, fund-raising, or educational use.

For details, contact:
DK Publishing Special Markets, 1450 Broadway, Suite 801,
New York, New York 10018
SpecialSales@dk.com

Printed in China

A WORLD OF IDEAS:
SEE ALL THERE IS TO KNOW

www.dk.com

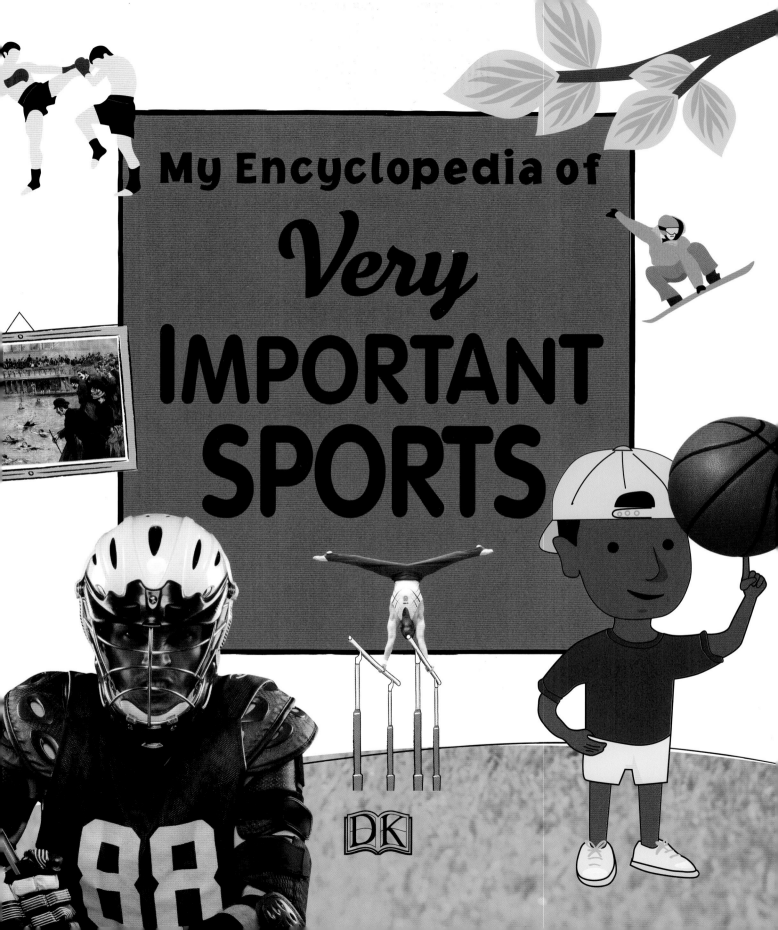

My Encyclopedia of
Very
IMPORTANT SPORTS

DK

Contents

 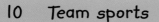

Amazing athletes

Sporting events

Sports

One of the best things about sports is how many **different ones** there are. There are sports played in the snow, in the water, on a special track, or just in the park. There really is a sport for everyone to enjoy, so lace up your sneakers and race to find your favorite. **Ready**, **set**, **go**!

Football

Volleyball

Netball

Basketball

Lacrosse

Handball

Baseball

Hockey

Soccer

Team sports

Playing on a team is a lot of fun, and team sports are a great way to make friends and develop skills, such as working **together**. Whether it's throwing, catching, hitting a ball, or scoring goals, the aim in these sports is simple—outscore the other team!

Aussie rules football

Cricket

Rugby

Soccer

Known as the "beautiful game," soccer, or football, is the world's most **popular sport**. It's played all over the globe, and its most famous tournament, the World Cup, is the planet's biggest sporting event.

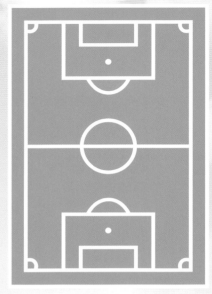

Soccer field

Simple game

The beauty of soccer is simplicity. Two teams of 11 players play on a field with a **goal** at each end. The aim is to kick a ball into the other team's goal. The team with the most goals at the end wins.

Goal

Goalkeeper

Goalkeepers defend the goals. They are the only players who are allowed to touch the ball with their hands.

Inventing the beautiful game

A game similar to soccer, called **Cuju**, was played in China more than 2,000 years ago, but the modern game started in England in the 19th century.

FACT FILE   Type of sport: Ball

The great thing about soccer is that it can be played anywhere by anyone. All you need is a ball!

The World Cup

The World Cup decides which country has the best team in the world. It takes place every four years, and the final is watched by **almost half the people on Earth**!

Although professional soccer is played by teams of 11, the game can be played for fun by any number of players.

Three-time World Cup winner Pelé, from Brazil, is one of the game's legends. He scored more than 1,000 goals in his career.

Players per team: 11

Equipment: Ball

Football

In the United States, football is played in school, at college, and professionally in the National Football League (NFL). Each year, the 32 NFL teams square off to win the big prize: the **Super Bowl**.

Posts

Defensive back

Wide receiver

Four downs

Teams take turns trying to get the ball in the other team's **end zone** at the end of the field. They get four chances, called **downs**, to move the ball 10 yards by either throwing it or running with it. If the attacking team (the offense) gains 10 yards, it gets four more downs. If it fails, the other team gets the ball.

FACT FILE   Type of sport:    Ball

Touchdown!

Teams score six points if they run the ball into the other team's end zone, or successfully catch the ball there. This is called a **touchdown**. Teams also score three points if they kick the ball between the posts for a **field goal**.

The quarterback is the most important player on a team. They organize the offensive players and throw the ball.

Football players wear lots of **pads** and a helmet to protect them when they get tackled.

Quarterback

The football is nicknamed a "pigskin."

Professional teams have 53 players on a team, but only 11 on each side play at once.

More pizza is sold in the United States on the day of the Super Bowl than on any other day of the year!

Players per team: 11

Equipment: Protective gear, helmet, ball

Australian rules football

Australian rules football is a very physical ball sport popular in **Australia**. It's played between two teams of 18 players.

The game can be rough, and players don't wear pads or a helmet, so need to be very tough.

Scoring

Teams move a ball around a big field by kicking it, running and bouncing it, or thumping it with their fists. They score points by kicking the ball between goal posts—**six points** for the middle posts and **one point** for the wider "behind" posts.

The game is also known as "Aussie rules" or just "footy."

FACT FILE

Type of sport: Ball

Even though women's games have been played since the 1910s, the official women's league only played its first season in 2017.

Instead of starting with a kickoff, matches start with an umpire bouncing the ball in the air. A player from each team tries to catch the ball and get it to their teammates.

The sport was invented as a game for cricketers to play during winter when the weather wasn't good enough for cricket.

	Goals	Behinds	Points
Team 1	11	14	80
Team 2	10	7	67

Australian rules football is played on an oval field

Funny scoring

A scoreboard might read: 11.14 (80), 10.7 (67). This means that Team 1 scored 80 points (11 goals and 14 behinds), while Team 2 scored 67 points (10 goals and 7 behinds).

Players per team: 18

Equipment: Ball

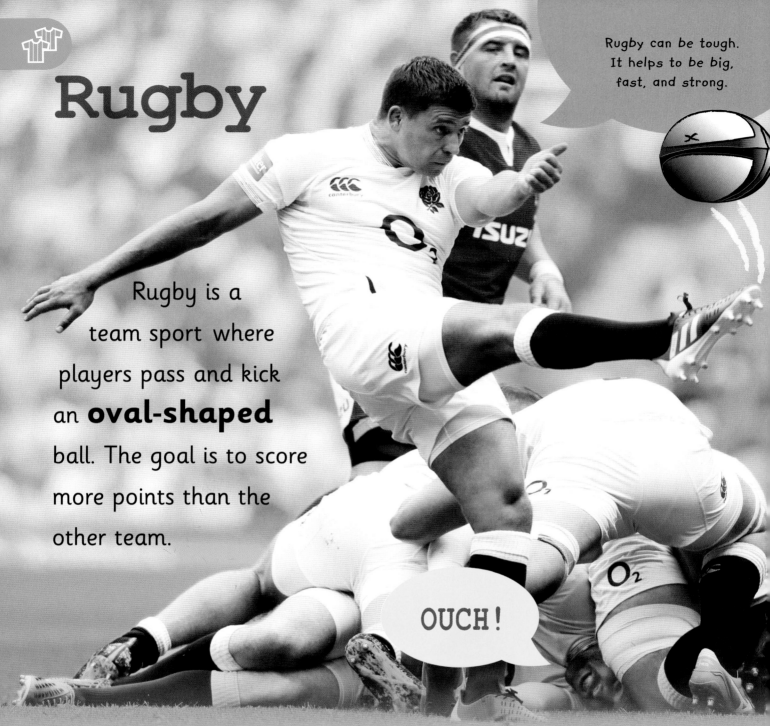

Rugby

Rugby can be tough. It helps to be big, fast, and strong.

Rugby is a team sport where players pass and kick an **oval-shaped** ball. The goal is to score more points than the other team.

OUCH!

Teams move the ball by passing it to a teammate or by kicking it. Players are only allowed to pass the ball backward. The defending team tackles players to take the ball from them.

If a team places the ball on the ground behind the other team's "try line," it scores a "try" and earns points. Teams also score points if they kick the ball between the goalposts.

FACT FILE   Type of sport: Ball

15 **Rugby union** is a 15-a-side version of the game. According to myth, it started in 1823, when a pupil at a school in Rugby, England, picked up the ball during a game of soccer and ran with it.

13 **Rugby league** is similar to rugby union, but teams have 13 players and the points for scoring are different.

7 **Sevens** is a seven-a-side version of rugby union. A match is made up of two halves lasting for seven minutes.

If a player passes the ball forward, a "scrum" occurs. In a scrum, the teams lock shoulders and push against each other. The ball is rolled into the middle and both teams struggle to get it.

After a try is scored, the team tries to kick the ball between the goalposts to earn more points. That's why it's called a "try."

Players per team:  7-15   Equipment: Rugby ball

Lacrosse

Lacrosse is a team sport where players **run**, **pass** a ball, **catch** it, and score using **sticks** with a net at the end.

Lacrosse stick

Body checking

Lacrosse is similar to many team sports in that the point is to **score goals** in the other team's net. When the other team has the ball, one way to get it back is to "body check" a player so they drop the ball. This means slamming into them!

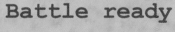

Battle ready

Lacrosse is based on a game played in Native American communities. It was used as a way to **prepare warriors for battle**. The game could last for days and sometimes included up to 1,000 players!

FACT FILE   Type of sport: Stick and ball

Body checking is only allowed in games of older players.

Fast and furious

Lacrosse is a very tough and physical sport. Players need to be covered in **protective gear**, including a helmet, shoulder pads, gloves, arm pads, and body armor.

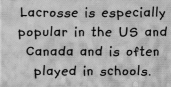

Lacrosse is especially popular in the US and Canada and is often played in schools.

Baseball

Baseball is played between two teams of nine players who take turns **batting** and **fielding**. It's hugely popular in North America, Japan, and South Korea.

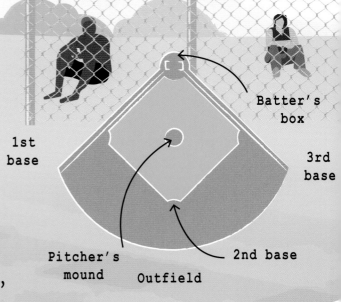

Batter's box

1st base

3rd base

Pitcher's mound

Outfield

2nd base

A baseball field is called a "diamond" because of its shape.

Batter up!

The game starts when **the pitcher** throws the ball toward the **batter**. The batter tries to hit the ball and sprint around **four bases** to score a **run**. It's the fielding team's job to get the batter out.

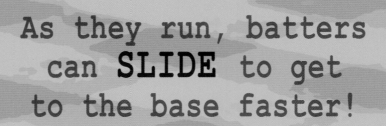

As they run, batters can **SLIDE** to get to the base faster!

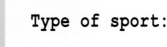

FACT FILE   Type of sport: Bat and ball

Three strikes and you're out!

Home run glory

If a player hits the ball out of the field, it's a home run. This means the player can run freely around **all four bases** to score.

Out!

There are a few ways the fielders can get a **batter out**:

 If the pitcher throws three strikes (makes the batter miss the ball three times).

If a fielder catches the ball before it touches the ground.

If the ball is thrown to a fielder standing on a base before the batter reaches it.

Baseball glove

Over 21 million hot dogs were eaten at baseball stadiums in the US in 2014.

Players per team: 9

Equipment:

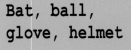 Bat, ball, glove, helmet

Cricket

Cricket is a bat-and-ball game popular in many countries. The aim of the game is to score more **runs** than the other team.

Fielders are a team's defenders. It's their job to catch the batsmen "out."

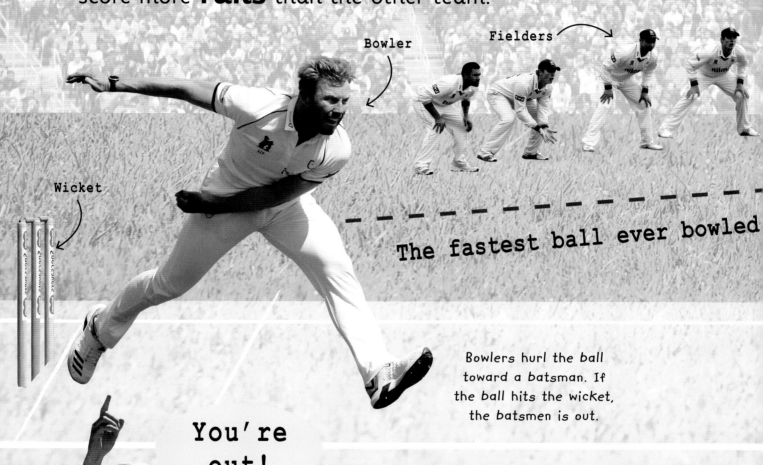

Bowler

Fielders

Wicket

The fastest ball ever bowled

Bowlers hurl the ball toward a batsman. If the ball hits the wicket, the batsmen is out.

You're out!

Two umpires make sure the match is fair and decide whether a batsman is out.

Cricket field
The game is played on a big field, in the center of which is a "pitch," which has **wickets** at both ends.

FACT FILE   Type of sport:    Bat and ball

One of cricket's biggest rivalries is between England and Australia. They play for a tiny trophy called "The Ashes." It's the smallest trophy in sports!

Aim of the game

One team scores runs when one of its batsmen **strikes the ball** with the bat. It's the other team's job to **get the batsman out**. There are lots of ways to do this, including catching a hit ball before it touches the ground.

Bat

Wicket

was at 100mph (160kph).

Pads

Ball

Cricket is extremely popular in India, Pakistan, and the West Indies.

Players per team: 11

Equipment: Bat, ball, wicket, pads, and helmet

Hockey

Hockey, also called field hockey, is a game where players use curved, **wooden sticks** to hit a ball to their teammates and try to **score goals**.

Matches are usually played on artificial

Players can only hit the ball with the flat side of the stick.

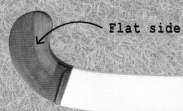

Flat side

FACT FILE   Type of sport: Stick and ball

Players are not allowed to touch the ball with their hands or feet.

Goalkeepers wear protective padding from head to toe.

The Wizard

India's **Dhyan Chand** is one of the greatest hockey players ever. He was known as **"The Wizard"** because of his amazing control of the ball. His team dominated men's hockey in the 1920s and 1930s and won three Olympic golds in a row between 1928 and 1936.

Origins

From ancient Greece to ancient China, games in which a ball is hit with a stick have been played for a very long time. But hockey as we know it developed in **Scotland** around 300 years ago.

Shinty is an old Scottish game similar to hockey.

Handle

grass because it's smoother than real grass.

Players per team: 11

Equipment: Hockey stick and ball

Basketball

Fast-paced and exciting, basketball is a popular team sport where two teams compete to shoot a ball into **baskets**.

Basket

The first basketball hoops were baskets peaches were sold in!

Basketball court

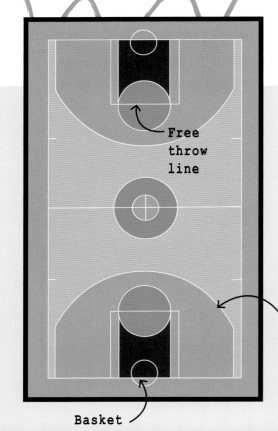

Free throw line

Three point line

Basket

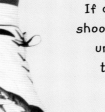

If a player is fouled while shooting, their team is given undefended shots from the "free throw" line.

FACT FILE

Type of sport: Ball

Shoot!

Getting the ball through the hoop earns points. Shots from outside the **three point line** are worth three points, and scores from inside it are worth two.

Michael Jordan is basketball's biggest legend. He averaged 30.1 points a game during his career.

Slam dunk in action!

Leaping and slamming the *ball* into the basket is called a slam dunk.

The world's most famous basketball league, the NBA, is in the United States, but basketball is popular across Europe and Asia, too.

Average man's shoe size

Basketball players are fast, skillful, and big. NBA legend Shaquille O'Neal is 7ft 1in (2.16m) tall and wears size 22 shoes!

Shaquille O'Neal's shoe size

A basketball is the largest ball used in any sport.

Netball

Netball is a team sport similar to basketball. Players pass a ball to each other and try to **shoot the ball** through one of two raised hoops at each end of the court.

It's the goalkeeper's job to protect their team's goal.

Beginning of the sport

Netball began as a version of basketball that was played by women **students** at a college in London. The first rules were made in 1901 and the sport grew from there.

The Netball World Cup is the sport's biggest event. Australia has won 11 times and never finished lower than second place.

FACT FILE   Type of sport:    Ball

Only the goal attack and goal shooter are allowed to enter the other team's goal circle and try to score.

Goal circle

Players are given positions that define what their job on the team is. Only some positions are allowed to go to certain parts of the court.

Rules of netball

The point of netball is to get the ball into the other team's hoop.

1 Players have letters on them to show the positions they take on the court.

2 Players are not allowed to run with or bounce the ball. They must pass the ball or shoot within three seconds of receiving it.

3 Shots can only be made from inside a special area called the goal circle. Only the goal attack and goal shooter can enter the area.

4 Defenders must stay at least 3ft (1m) away from a player who has the ball.

5 Matches last for 60 minutes. The team with the most goals at the end of the game wins.

GK	GD	WD	C	WA	GA	GS
Goal keeper	Goal defense	Wing defense	Center	Wing attack	Goal attack	Goal Shooter

60 mins

Volleyball

Volleyball is played between two teams separated by a **tall net**. The teams hit the ball over the net until one team can't return it.

Indoor volleyball has been played at the Olympics since the 1964 Games in Tokyo, Japan.

Teaching volleyball

Volleyball was invented by American teacher William G. Morgan in 1895. He combined parts of **tennis**, **handball**, and **basketball** to create a game that would keep his students fit.

Volleyball is played regularly by more than 800 million people around the world.

Most volleyball players jump around 300 times during a match.

FACT FILE   Type of sport:    Ball

Over the net

Teams knock the ball back and forth over the net. Each team can touch the ball **three times** before returning it, but players are not allowed to touch the ball twice in a row. If the ball touches the ground, or a team fails to return the ball into the opponent's court, the other team scores a point.

"Jenny" Lang Ping of China is a volleyball legend as both a player and a coach.

After retiring as a player, I coached the Chinese and US teams.

Net

Beach volleyball

Beach volleyball is a **two-a-side** version of volleyball played on sand. It has been played at the Olympic Games since 1996.

Handball

Handball is a fast-paced ball game played between two teams of seven players. The goal is to move the ball around the field and **throw it** into the other team's goal.

Handball is very popular in Europe. Especially in France, Germany, Spain, and Sweden.

The game's first rules were written in 1906 by Danish sports teacher and Olympian Holger Nielsen.

Moving around

To move the ball, players can **pass** it to each other, **run** with it, or **shoot!**

If a player runs with the ball, they must bounce it as they run (dribble with it).

Dribbling

Passing

World Championships

The handball World Championships are held every two years. **France** has won the men's event six times, and **Russia** holds the record in the women's, with four wins.

Scoring goals

The goal is surrounded by a 20ft (6m) **zone**, in which only the goalkeeper is allowed. Goals have to be scored from outside the zone or while jumping into it.

FACT FILE

Type of sport:
Ball

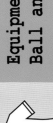

Players per team: 7

Equipment:
Ball and goal

35

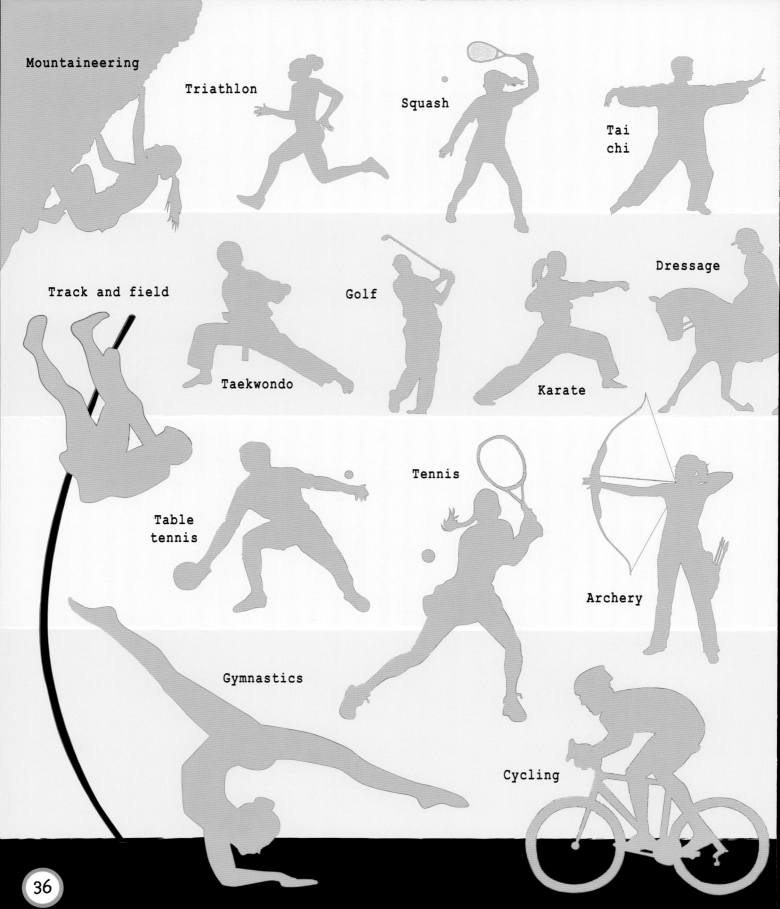

Mountaineering

Triathlon

Squash

Tai chi

Track and field

Taekwondo

Golf

Karate

Dressage

Table tennis

Tennis

Archery

Gymnastics

Cycling

Individual sports

There are lots of solo sports to choose from, and they all require very different **skills**. Players mostly compete on their own, but some solo sports can be played in pairs or as a small team. Hop, skip, and jump over the page to learn more.

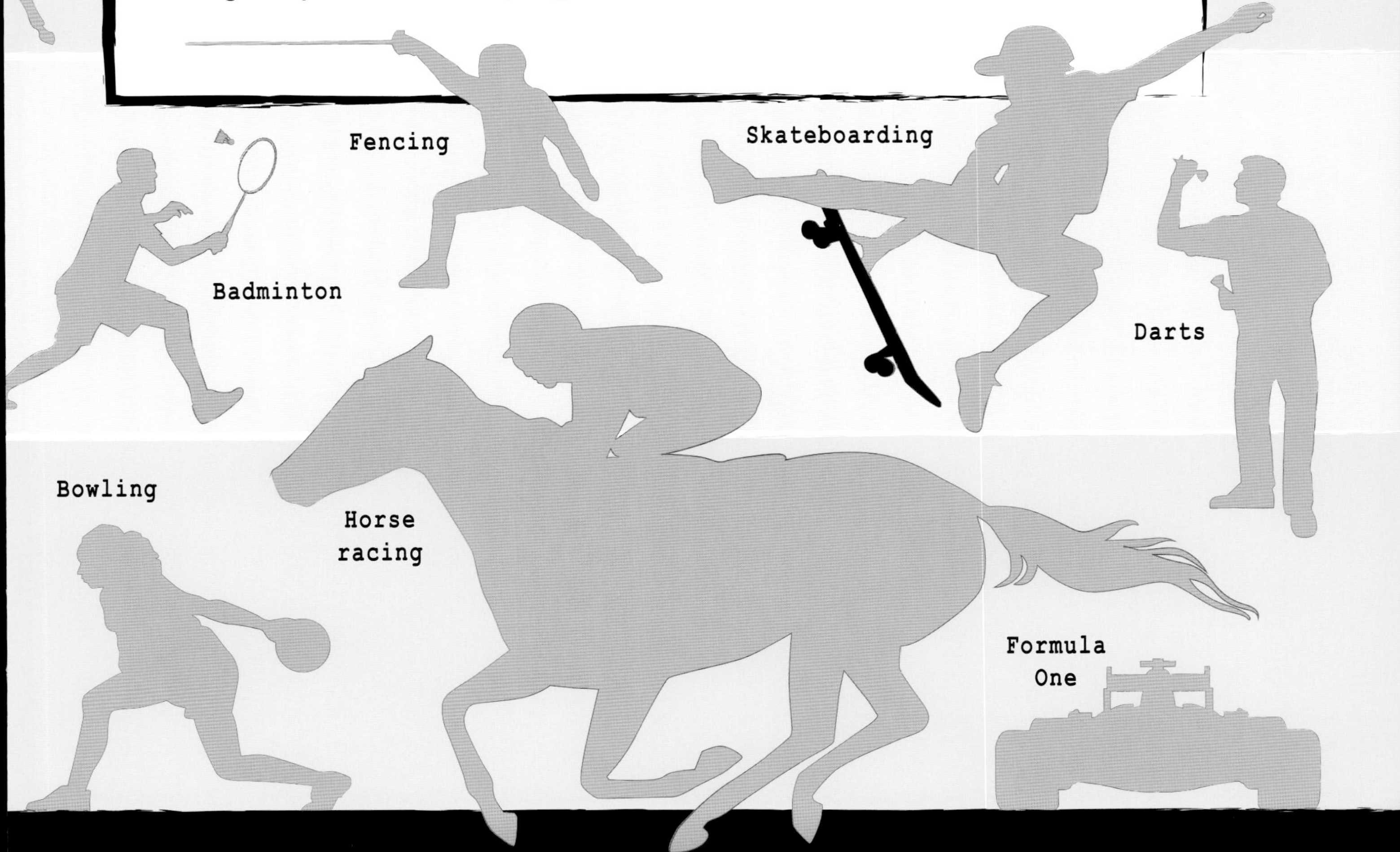

Snooker

Fencing

Skateboarding

Badminton

Darts

Bowling

Horse racing

Formula One

Ancient sports

People have played sports since ancient times, as a way of having fun and as competition. Some ancient sports are **still played today**!

Kabaddi

This game is played by two teams of seven. One player, known as the "raider," runs into the other team's half of the court, tags as many opponents as possible, and gets back to their own half without being tackled.

Polo

First played in Persia (now Iran) in the sixth century BCE, polo is one of the world's oldest team sports. Players on horses use a hammer to try and hit a ball into an opponent's goal.

Pitch-pot

In this ancient game from East Asia, players try to throw long sticks or arrows into a jar or pot from a distance.

Wrestling

This combat sport is all about overpowering the opponent by grappling, throwing, and pinning them down. It was painted on cave walls 15,000 years ago and is still played today!

Jousting

In this medieval sport, two riders charge at each other on horseback while holding a long stick called a "lance." The aim is to knock your opponent off their horse.

Nguni stick-fighting

In this ancient African martial art, two players fight each other with two sticks. One stick is used to attack; the purpose of the other is to defend.

Episkyros

In this ancient Greek ball game, players pass a ball to a teammate standing behind the other team's goal line. It's a little like football in the US.

Chunkey

This Native American game was first played 1,500 years ago. One player rolls a stone disk across the ground, while others throw spears and try to hit it.

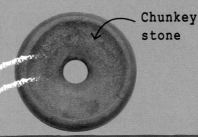

Chunkey stone

Cuju

Played in China from the third century BCE, this sport is thought to be one of the earliest forms of soccer.

Running

From fast sprints to long-distance endurance races, there are lots of running events in track and field. Running short distances requires explosive **speed**; athletes who run long distances need energy and **stamina**.

Sprints and distances

The distances for running at the **Olympics** are divided into sprints, middle-distance races, and long-distance races. They are:

100m	200m	400m	800m
The shortest running event takes place on the straight section of a running track. Jamaica's Usain Bolt broke the world record in 2009.	Athletes start the 200m race on the curve of a track and finish on a straight. American Florence Griffith-Joyner set the women's record in 1988 and it's never been beaten.	This race takes place around a full lap of the track. Runners either start quickly and try to keep a good pace, or increase their speed near the end.	The shortest of the middle-distance races, the 800m requires both stamina and speed. Athletes run two laps of the track.
Usain Bolt	Florence Griffith-Joyner		David Rudisha

Current world records

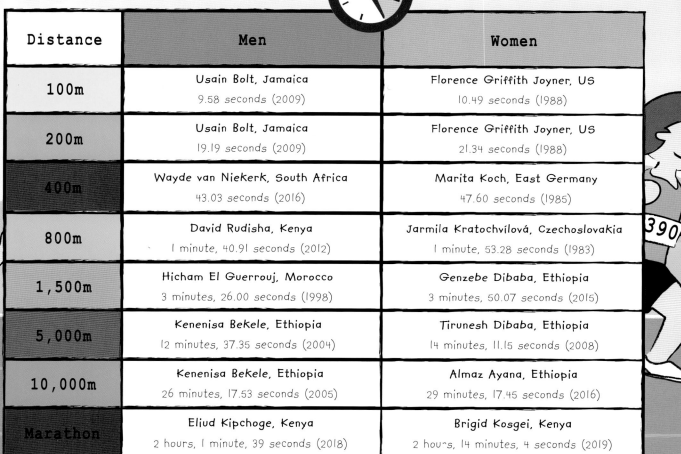

Distance	Men	Women
100m	Usain Bolt, Jamaica 9.58 seconds (2009)	Florence Griffith Joyner, US 10.49 seconds (1988)
200m	Usain Bolt, Jamaica 19.19 seconds (2009)	Florence Griffith Joyner, US 21.34 seconds (1988)
400m	Wayde van Niekerk, South Africa 43.03 seconds (2016)	Marita Koch, East Germany 47.60 seconds (1985)
800m	David Rudisha, Kenya 1 minute, 40.91 seconds (2012)	Jarmila Kratochvílová, Czechoslovakia 1 minute, 53.28 seconds (1983)
1,500m	Hicham El Guerrouj, Morocco 3 minutes, 26.00 seconds (1998)	Genzebe Dibaba, Ethiopia 3 minutes, 50.07 seconds (2015)
5,000m	Kenenisa Bekele, Ethiopia 12 minutes, 37.35 seconds (2004)	Tirunesh Dibaba, Ethiopia 14 minutes, 11.15 seconds (2008)
10,000m	Kenenisa Bekele, Ethiopia 26 minutes, 17.53 seconds (2005)	Almaz Ayana, Ethiopia 29 minutes, 17.45 seconds (2016)
Marathon	Eliud Kipchoge, Kenya 2 hours, 1 minute, 39 seconds (2018)	Brigid Kosgei, Kenya 2 hours, 14 minutes, 4 seconds (2019)

1,500m

This race covers three-and-a-quarter laps of a track. The best athletes run the race as a long sprint.

Hicham El Guerrouj

5,000m

This is the shortest long-distance race and covers 12-and-a-half laps of a track.

Kenenisa Bekele

10,000m

Athletes must complete 25 laps of the track. The event has been part of the Olympics for men since 1912. Women have completed in the event since 1988.

Almaz Ayana

Marathon

The marathon is the longest event. Instead of running on a track, athletes race over a road course that is 26.219 miles (42.195km) long.

Brigid Kosgei

Hurdles

Four track and field events involve jumping over **obstacles**. Women run the 100m hurdles, while men run 110m. Both compete in a 400m hurdles race and a 3,000m steeplechase, which has special obstacles.

Steeplechase is the human version of a type of horse race. Obstacles include tall barriers and water pits.

The hurdles are set at different heights, depending on the race.

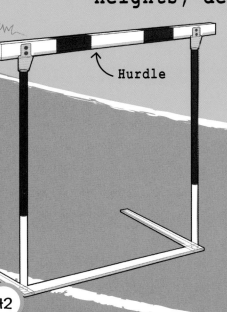

Hurdle

42in (106.7cm) for the men's 110m and 36in (91.44cm) for the men's 400m.

33in (83.8cm) for the women's 100m and 30in (76.2cm) for the women's 400m.

36in (91.4cm) in the men's steeplechase and 30in (76.2cm) in women's.

42

Master hurdler

American Ed Moses was top of the men's 400m hurdles for a decade. He won **122 races in a row** between 1977 and 1987, picking up four world records and two Olympic gold medals.

World records

Distance	Men	Women
100m hurdles	No event	Kendra Harrison, US 12.20 seconds (2016)
110m hurdles	Aries Merritt, US 12.80 seconds (2012)	No event
400m hurdles	Kevin Young, US 46.78 seconds (1992)	Dalilah Muhammad, US 52.16 seconds (2019)
3,000m steeplechase	Saif Saaeed Shaheen, Qatar 7 minutes, 53.63 seconds (2004)	Beatrice Chepkoech, Kenya 8 minutes, 44.32 seconds (2018)

Top long jumpers leap farther than a London bus!

Jumps

In track and field, there are four events where **jumping** is key: long jump, high jump, triple jump, and pole vault.

High jump

Flip

Athletes jump over a bar onto a mat. If they clear the bar, it is moved higher. If they don't clear it in three tries, they are eliminated. The winner is whoever jumps highest.

Long jump

Leap

In long jump, athletes sprint down a runway then leap as far as they can into a sand pit. The winner is whoever leaps farthest.

Triple jump

Hop...

Skip...

44

World records

Event	Men	Women
High jump	Javier Sotomayor, Cuba 2.45m (1993)	Stefka Kostadinova, Bulgaria 2.09m (1987)
Long jump	Mike Powell, US 8.95m (1991)	Galina Chistyakova, USSR 7.52m (1988)
Triple jump	Jonathan Edwards, GB 18.29m (1995)	Inessa Kravets, Ukraine 15.50m (1995)
Pole vault	Renaud Lavillenie, France 6.16m (2014)	Yelena Isinbayeva, Russia 5.06m (2009)

Pole vault

Just as in high jump, pole vaulters have to leap over a bar. But they use a long stick to help them off the ground and over the bar.

Ukraine's Sergey Bubka broke the pole vault world record 35 times between 1984 and 2001!

Sergey Bubka

Jump

Triple jump is similar to the long jump, but athletes must hop, skip, then jump. The winner is the athlete who gets the farthest.

Throws

There are four throwing events in track and field:
shot put, **discus**, **javelin**, and **hammer**.
In each event, the athlete who throws the farthest wins.

Discus

Shot

Shot put

Athletes throw a small, heavy metal ball, called a **shot**, as far as they can, while staying inside a special throwing circle.

Discus is an ancient sport. There are statues of people throwing a discus that date back more than 2,000 years.

Discus

Athletes spin around to gain speed, then throw a **metal disk** (the discus) as far as possible. As with shot put, competitors have to stay in a special circle while throwing.

Javelin

Javelin is the only throwing event in which athletes don't stay in a throwing circle. They sprint down a runway and release the javelin (a **spear**) through the air.

Hammer

Hammer

The hammer isn't like a hammer you would find in a toolbox. It's a **metal ball** attached to a steel wire. Athletes spin around in a throwing circle, build up speed, then let it go.

Javelin

Shot put

Hammer

Javelin

Discus

Event	Men	Women
Shot put	Randy Barnes, US 23.12m (1990)	Natalya Lisovskaya, USSR 22.63m (1987)
Discus	Jürgen Schult, East Germany 74.08m (1986)	Gabriele Reinsch, East Germany 76.80m (1988)
Javelin	Jan Železný, Czech Republic 98.48m (1996)	Barbora Špotáková, Czech Republic 72.28m (2008)
Hammer	Yuriy Sedykh, USSR 86.74m (1986)	Anita Włodarczyk, Poland 82.98m (2016)

Combined events

Combined events are the **ultimate test** of an athlete's abilities, as the competition includes many events to decide the winner. Men compete in the **decathlon**, while women compete in the **heptathlon**.

Decathlon world record
Kevin Mayer, France
9,126 points (2018)

Decathlon
The decathlon has **10 events**:

| 100m | Long jump | Shot put | High jump | 400m |

| 110m hurdles | Discus | Pole vault | 1,500m | Javelin |

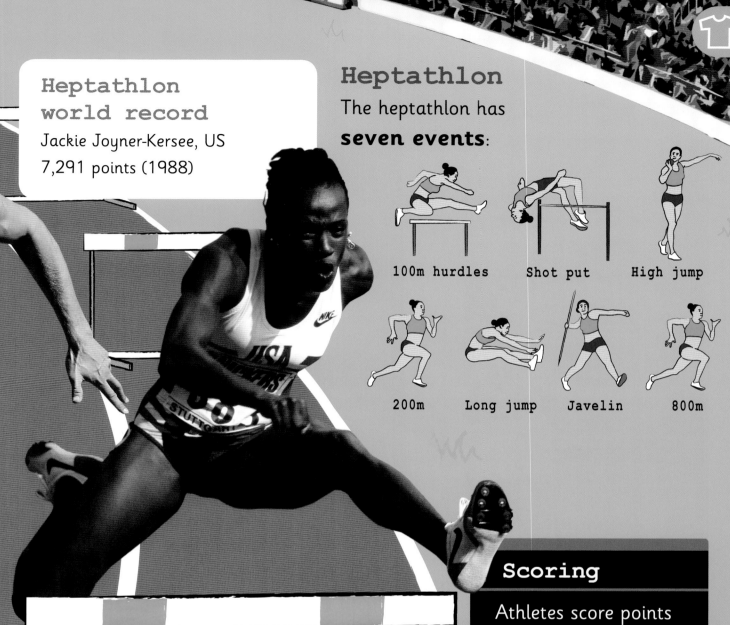

Heptathlon world record

Jackie Joyner-Kersee, US
7,291 points (1988)

Heptathlon

The heptathlon has **seven events**:

100m hurdles   Shot put   High jump

200m   Long jump   Javelin   800m

The heptathlon was first part of the OLYMPIC GAMES in 1984.

Scoring

Athletes score points for the time, height, or distance they achieve in each event. The points are added up and the athlete with the most points at the end wins.

49

Triathlon

A triathlon is an endurance race where athletes **swim**, **cycle**, then **run**, one after the other. People who take part in triathlons must train very hard!

How it all started

Multisport events have been around since ancient times, but **no one really knows** the origins of the modern triathlon. However, the first official swim-cycle-run competition was held in the US in 1974, and it was the first to be officially called a triathlon.

Triathlon is a mix of two Greek words, "tri" and "athlos," which mean "three competitions."

Olympic triathlon

Triathlon became an Olympic event at the 2000 Olympics in Sydney, Australia. Competitors complete a 0.93 mile (1.5km) swim, followed by a 25 mile (40km) cycle, then a 6.2 mile (10km) run.

FACT FILE   Type of sport: Endurance

Exceptional athlete

Britain's Alistair Brownlee is the only triathlete in history to win **back to back** Olympic titles. He won gold at the 2012 Games in London, England, and then again in Rio de Janeiro, Brazil, four years later.

← Alistair Brownlee

There are variations of the classic triathlon. One features cross-country skiing, mountain biking, and running.

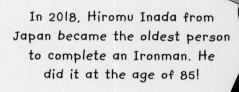

In 2018, Hiromu Inada from Japan became the oldest person to complete an Ironman. He did it at the age of 85!

Made of iron

There are several extreme versions of triathlons. The most famous is called an **Ironman**. In this race, competitors swim 2.4 miles (3.9km), cycle 112 miles (180km), and then run 26.2 miles (42.2 km).

The record for an Ironman is held by Germany's Jan Frodeno. He completed the event in 7 hours, 35 minutes, 39 seconds.

Number of players: 1

Equipment: Running shoes, swimwear, bicycle

Gymnastics

Gymnasts make incredibly difficult **acrobatics** look effortless. There are lots of events, but they all require strength, flexibility, balance, and stamina.

Balance beam

Gymnasts perform jumps, flips, and twists on a thin wooden beam without falling off.

Beam

Pommel horse

The pommel horse is a box with handles on it. Gymnasts use the horse to spin on their hands, do scissor kicks, and handstands.

Most gymnasts start training when they are very young.

Uneven bars

Without touching the floor, gymnasts spin, do handstands and jumps on two bars set at different heights.

Floor exercise

Gymnasts show their acrobatic skills on a spring floor mat by performing balances, jumps, flips, leaps, and turns.

 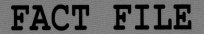

Gymnastics has appeared at every Olympics since 1896. Men and women compete in slightly different events.

Parallel bars

Gymnasts use two bars to perform a series of swings, balances, and spins.

Rings

Gymnasts lift themselves off the ground on the rings and use their strength to spin and hold different positions.

Vault

After a short run-up, gymnasts jump onto a springboard, place their hands on a vault, throw themselves up into the air, and perform flips.

Trampolining

In trampolining, gymnasts bounce in the air as they spin and twirl. Competitions can be for one gymnast or pairs.

Rhythmic gymnastics

This is a mix of dance, gymnastics, and ballet. Rhythmic gymnasts perform routines with props such as balls, hoops, ribbons, clubs, or a jump rope.

Number of players: 1-4

Equipment: Beam, pommel horse, bars, rings, and more

53

Cycling

People ride bikes for fun or to get around, but competitive cycling takes it up a level. There are lots of different races that take place on **roads** or on indoor tracks called **velodromes**.

Cycling's biggest races are known as the "Grand Tours." The most well-known, the Tour de France, lasts for three weeks!

Cycling races can be quick sprints or endurance races that take a long time and lots of stamina.

SPRINT RACES

SPRINT

These races are mostly between two cyclists who race over a set distance, usually between 250m–1,000m.

TEAM SPRINT

This is a three-person team time trial. Teams try to record the fastest time.

KEIRIN

In this six-lap race, riders have to stay behind a motorcycle for the first three laps. They are then released to race over the last three.

TIME TRIAL

Each rider tries to record the fastest time over a set distance.

ENDURANCE RACES

INDIVIDUAL PURSUIT

Two cyclists start on opposite ends of a track. If one rider catches the other, the race is over. If neither catches the other, the one with the fastest time wins.

SCRATCH RACE

In this race, all the riders start together and race. The winner is the first to cross the finish line.

(54) **FACT FILE**   Type of sport: Cycling

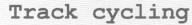

Road races

Single cyclists or teams take part in races on roads. Some are staged over **several laps** of a course, some take a day, and others are **multistage** races that take much longer.

Track cycling

Track cycling events take place in specially built velodromes. The tracks usually have two flat straights with slanted turns at either end to help the cyclists go **faster**.

TEAM PURSUIT

Just as in the individual pursuit, cyclists chase each other around a track, but in teams of up to four riders.

MADISON

This is a team-relay event. The winning team is the one that completes the most laps in a set time.

MISS AND OUT

This is an elimination race in which the slowest riders are eliminated until only the winner is left.

POINTS RACE

These can be complicated to watch. A sprint is held every 10 laps and the first five riders in each sprint collect points. The rider with the most points wins.

OMNIUM

This is a multistage event, involving several kinds of race in one. The winner is the rider who gets the most overall points.

Number of players: 1 or team

Equipment: Bicycle, helmet

Formula One

Formula One is a fast, thrilling racing sport. Drivers race and are awarded points for the position they finish in. The driver with the most points at the end of the season is the **champion**.

A Formula One car can cost $10 million!

← Monaco Grand Prix

Fast-paced racing

Races are called "Grand Prix," which means **"large prize"** in French. Each Grand Prix is held on a different track, which can vary a lot. For example, the Monaco Grand Prix is held around twisty streets, while the Italian Grand Prix has long straights to speed down.

FACT FILE   Type of sport: Motor

I won seven world titles between 1994 and 2004.

Germany's Michael Schumacher is the most successful driver in the history of the sport.

Pit stops

During races, drivers pull into special "pit stops" where a team changes all their tyres in seconds! A good pit stop makes the difference between **winning and losing** the race.

Pit stop

Officials wave a checkered flag to show when the winner crosses the finish line.

Built for speed

Formula One cars can reach speeds of 235 mph (375 kph). They are specially designed to generate **downforce**, which helps them stay on the ground when they go around corners at such high speeds.

Motor sports

There are lots of sports where man and machine come together with one goal in mind: going as **fast as possible**!

↑
Lewis
Hamilton

Go-karting

Many Formula One drivers, such as Lewis Hamilton, start off racing go-karts. Drivers race around tracks in small powerful karts.

Touring car racing

Drivers race everyday cars that have been modified around race tracks. Some touring car races last a whole day!

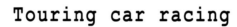

Motorcycle racing

Riders drive high-powered motorcycles around tracks or road circuits at super speeds.

Drag racing

This is the ultimate test of speed. Drag racers drive cars designed to go as fast as possible in a straight line over a short distance.

Speedway

Between four to six riders race motorcycles around a short dirt track.

Monster truck

Monster trucks

These huge trucks race around tracks that have a number of jumps. Sometimes the trucks fly over cars or crush them!

Monster truck tires can be taller than people!

Rallying

As with touring car racing, rally cars are normal cars that have been modified. Instead of racing on tracks, they race on a road course.

NASCAR

NASCAR is one of the most popular motor sports in the US. Drivers race around tracks or street circuits in special cars called stock cars.

Stock car

Horse racing

Horse racing is one of the **oldest** sports there is. Riders called **jockeys** race horses around a track as fast as possible.

Flat races

In flat races, horses gallop around a **track**. Some of the world's most famous horse races, such as the Kentucky Derby, are flat races.

The Kentucky Derby is called the "Fastest Two Minutes in Sports."

Kentucky Derby

60 **FACT FILE**   Type of sport: Equestrian

Jump races

Also known as "steeplechase," jump races take place on a track, but horses must jump over **obstacles**, such as fences and ditches.

Steeplechase jump

Steeplechasing gets its name from races that took place between two church steeples.

Jockeys are SMALL AND LIGHT, so the horses can RUN FASTER.

Most races are run counterclockwise around the track.

Number of players:

1 rider per horse

Equipment: Helmet, saddle, bridle

Show jumping

Equestrian events are competitions for **horses** and **riders**. The most well-known is show jumping.

Show jumping

Show jumping is an **obstacle course** for horses and riders. Horses have to leap over hedges and walls. Riders lose points if their horse is too slow or knocks over an obstacle.

Neighhhh!

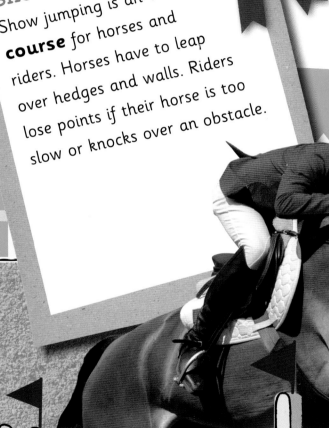

Jump

FACT FILE   Type of sport: Equestrian

Dressage hat

Dressage

Dressage horses perform **special steps** and moves to show how well they follow instructions from their rider.

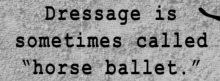

Aaaachoo!

British rider Lee Pearson has won 10 dressage gold medals at the Paralympics even though he is allergic to horses!

Dance steps

Dressage gets its name from the French word for **"training."** It takes a lot of time and skill to train a horse to be obedient enough for dressage. Some dressage events are performed to **music**, just like a dance.

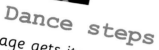

Dressage is sometimes called "horse ballet."

| Number of players: | 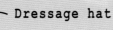 1 | Equipment: | Saddle, bridle, boots, protective hat |

Combat sports

There are lots of sports where opponents face each other in a **one-on-one** fight. Most were created years ago in different cultures around the world.

Boxing gloves

Kendo shinai

Krav Maga

This martial art was developed by the Israeli army. It is a mix of boxing, wrestling, aikido, judo, and karate.

Kendo

Kendo is a Japanese martial art where fighters wear protective armor and use bamboo swords called "shinai" to fight each other.

Judo

The goal in judo is to grapple and throw your opponent to the ground and pin them there. It was invented in Japan.

Boxing

Boxing is one of the world's oldest combat sports. It's also called pugilism. Boxers wear padded gloves on their hands.

POW

Even though they involve fighting, most martial arts

Ring

Sumo wrestling

Sumo wrestling is Japan's national sport. Wrestlers must force their opponents out of a ring or throw them to the ground to win.

Aikido

This Japanese martial art has its roots in the 12th century, but the modern form was developed in the early 20th century. It is mainly used for self-defense.

Hakama

Capoeira

This is an African-Brazilian martial art that developed in Brazil in the 16th century. It combines elements of dance, acrobatics, and music.

Kickboxing

Kickboxing developed as a mix of karate and boxing. There are lots of different styles from different countries.

Mixed martial arts

This sport uses techniques from many types of martial art. It combines grappling and striking.

Kung Fu

"Kung Fu" refers to the Chinese martial arts. Monks invented Kung Fu as a way to train their bodies for meditation.

are meant for self-defense.

Karate

Karate is a **martial art** (form of self-defense) that uses punching, kicking, and hand strikes. Karate originated on the Japanese island of Okinawa in the 19th century and later became a popular sport.

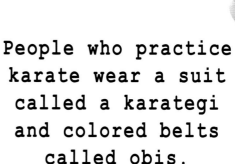

Karategi

Obi

> Someone who practices karate is known as a karateka.

People who practice karate wear a suit called a karategi and colored belts called obis.

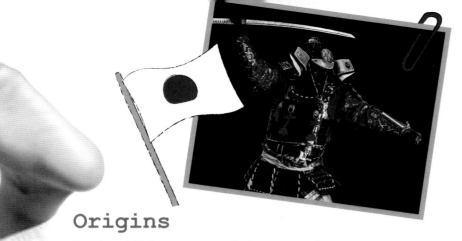

Origins

In the 17th century, fighting with weapons was banned on Okinawa, so its warriors came up with karate. The word karate means "**empty hand**."

Karate's popularity spread to the United States when Okinawa became an important US military base after World War II.

Gaining belts

As karateka improve at karate, they pass through several ranks (**dans**). Each dan has a different colored belt. Beginners start with white, and experts wear black.

Types of move

Karate is known for striking actions such as palm heel, knife hand, and spear hand strikes. But karate is mostly about self-defense and developing **balance** between the mind and body.

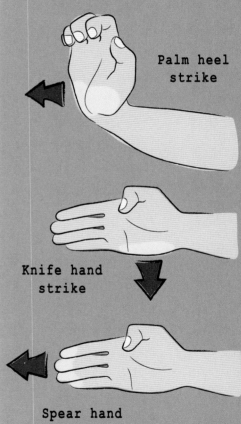

Palm heel strike

Knife hand strike

Spear hand strike

Number of players:

 2

Equipment:

Karate suit (karategi) and belt (obi)

Taekwondo

Taekwondo is a martial art and form of self-defense based on speed, agility, and acrobatic **kicks**.

Origins

Taekwondo developed in **South Korea** from a number of different Korean, Japanese, and Chinese martial arts that date back more than **2,000** years.

People who take part in Taekwondo are expected to follow the sport's five tenets (rules).

Courtesy
Integrity
Perseverance
Self-control
Indomitable spirit

"Tae" means foot, "kwon" means fist, and "do" translates to "art" or "the way."

The Taekwondo uniform is called a "DOBOK."

(68) FACT FILE   Type of sport: Martial art

Contestants perform in weight categories, so they always fight against someone who is similar to them in size.

Taekwondo first appeared at the Olympics in Sydney, Australia, in 2000. South Korea has won more medals than any other country.

Hogu

Competitions

Contestants wear a red or blue chest protector (called a **hogu**), a head guard, and other forms of protection. The contest is made up of **three rounds** of two minutes. The person who scores the most points wins.

3   How to win points   5

One point for a foot or fist strike that hits the body

Three points for a kick to the head

Three points for a spinning or backkick that strikes the body

Four points for a spinning kick to the head

Number of players: 2   Equipment: Dobok, helmet, hogu

Tai chi

This very old martial art uses slow **flowing movements**, deep breathing, and meditation to exercise the body and clear the mind.

Ancient art

Tai chi began in **China** hundreds of years ago. According to legend, a monk named Zhang Sanfeng came upon a fight between a snake and a bird. The way the animals moved inspired him to create tai chi.

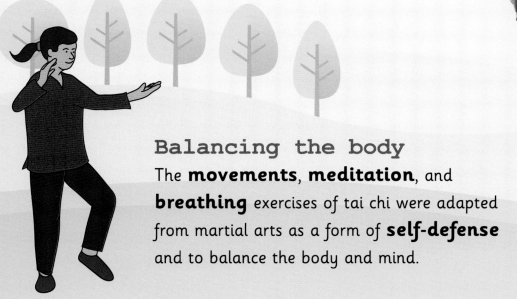

Balancing the body

The **movements**, **meditation**, and **breathing** exercises of tai chi were adapted from martial arts as a form of **self-defense** and to balance the body and mind.

FACT FILE   Type of sport: Martial art

More than 10 million people practice tai chi daily in China. It's one of the world's most popular ways to exercise.

There are five styles of tai chi. They are named after the five families who created them.

Routines

The type and **number of moves** in a tai chi routine depend on the style of tai chi. Some forms have around **20** movements, and others have up to **150**.

 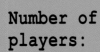

Fencing

Fencing is a safe version of **sword fighting**. It's based on the ancient art of swordsmanship, but the modern rules date back to 19th century Europe.

Protective clothing and mask

Fencers wear white because before electronic scoring, swords were dipped in ink to show when a hit had landed.

Dueling dancers

Fencers are fast, skilled, and move like dancers. There's a reason for this—**ballet** began as a dance version of fencing. Many of the movements are very similar.

72 **FACT FILE**   Type of sport:    Combat

Forms of fencing

There are three different forms of fencing, depending on the weapon being used: the **foil**, the **épée**, or the **saber**. The goal is the same in all of them—score points by touching the opponent with the sword.

Contact is detected electronically using a special cord. A sound is made or a light comes on when a touch is made.

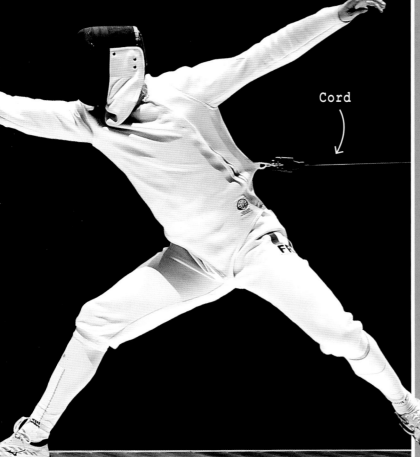

Cord

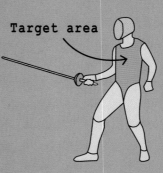

Foil

Target area

In foil, fencers score points by touching their opponent's chest with the tip of the sword.

Foil

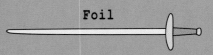

Épée

Target area

The épée is a slightly heavier weapon than the foil. Fencers score points by touching any part of their opponent's body with the tip.

Epee

Saber

Target area

In saber, fencers score by hitting any part of their opponent's upper body except the hands with the tip or blade of the sword.

Saber

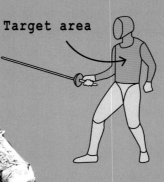

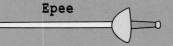

Number of players: 2

Equipment:  Sword and protective equipment

Tennis

Tennis is a racket sport where players take turns **hitting a ball** over a net into the other side of the court.

Players have to master several types of shot, including the serve, volley, forehand, backhand, and lob.

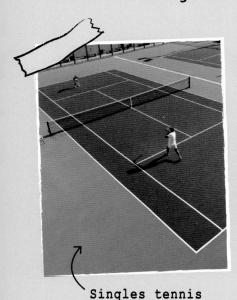

Singles tennis

Singles or doubles

Tennis can be played against one opponent, called "singles," or as a pair against two opponents, called "doubles." Singles games use **part** of the court and doubles games use the **whole** court.

Doubles tennis

Top tournaments

The four biggest tournaments in tennis are known as the "**Grand Slams**," or majors. These are Wimbledon, the French Open, the US Open, and the Australian Open.

If a player serves and their opponent

FACT FILE   Type of sport:    Racket

3	**1 0**	**2**
GAMES	SETS	GAMES

Game, Set, Match

Scoring in tennis can be a little tricky. Players win a **game** by scoring four points. However, if both players have scored three points, the game goes on until one player gains a lead of two points.

When a player wins six games, they win a **set**. But if the scores are tied at six games all, the players play a special game called a tiebreak.

Men play best of five sets and women play best of three. The overall winner wins the **match**.

The points are counted as "love" (0 points), 15 (1 point), 30 (2 points), and 40 (3 points). Nobody knows for sure how this system came about!

...an't hit the ball, it's called an "ACE."

Number of players: 2-4

Equipment: Racket and balls

Badminton

Badminton is a racket sport where players hit a **shuttlecock** (also called a "bird" or "birdie") over a **net**. Singles matches are played between two people, and doubles between four.

Racket

How to play

Players hit the shuttlecock over onto the other side of the net. Players then hit the shuttlecock back and forth until it **hits the ground**, the net, or goes out of the court.

Then and now

Although modern badminton came from Europe, it's most **popular in Asia**. It has been an Olympic sport since 1992, and Asian players have won by far the most medals.

Type of sport:  Racket

Shuttlecock

Strange-looking ball!

Shuttlecocks are made from overlapping feathers fixed to a cork base. They are usually plastic but can be made with **goose feathers**.

China's Lin Dan is widely thought of as the best badminton player ever.

Honk!

Badminton is the second most played sport in the world. It used to be called "battledore and shuttlecock."

Badminton court

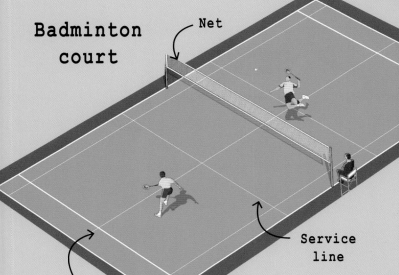

Net

Service line

Base line

Each player is only allowed to strike the shuttlecock once before it crosses the net.

Squash

Squash is a racket sport played on a court with walls. It's one of the **fastest** and most intense sports to play.

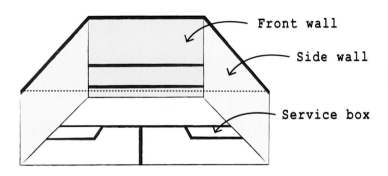

Front wall

Side wall

Service box

Aim of the game

Players serve from the service box, then take turns hitting the ball onto the **front wall** of the court. Players can **bounce** the ball off the side or back walls, just as long as it hits the front wall. The ball is only allowed to bounce on the ground **once**.

Scoring

Scoring systems vary, but usually the first player to win **11 points** wins the game (called a "set"). A match is usually made up of three or five sets.

Bouncing balls

Squash players choose their ball depending on their skill level. Each ball is marked by different colored **dots**.

Blue balls are best for beginners. They are fast-paced and have a very high bounce.

Red balls are medium-paced with a high bounce. They are mostly used by medium-level players.

Yellow balls are slow with a low bounce and are used by advanced players.

Double yellow balls are used by expert players. They are extra slow with a very low bounce.

FACT FILE Type of sport:  Racket

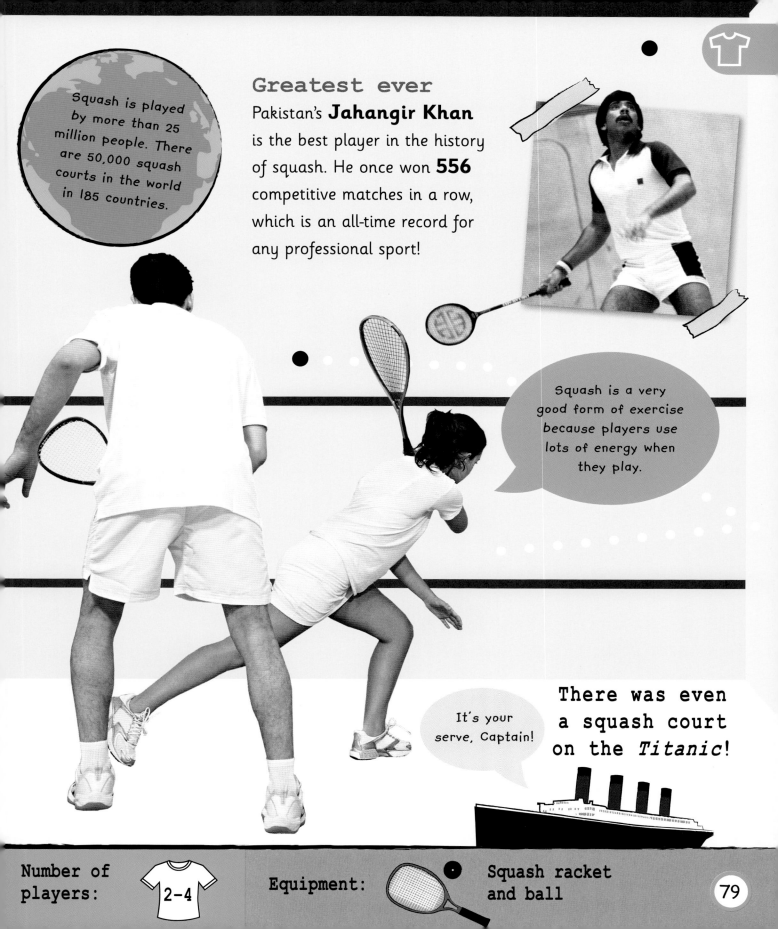

Greatest ever

Pakistan's **Jahangir Khan** is the best player in the history of squash. He once won **556** competitive matches in a row, which is an all-time record for any professional sport!

Squash is played by more than 25 million people. There are 50,000 squash courts in the world in 185 countries.

Squash is a very good form of exercise because players use lots of energy when they play.

It's your serve, Captain!

There was even a squash court on the *Titanic*!

Number of players: 2–4

Equipment: Squash racket and ball

Table tennis

Also known as "**ping pong**," table tennis is a lightning-quick racket sport where players use a wooden paddle to hit a ball back and forth across a table.

How to play

Players hit the ball over a net in the middle of the table so it **bounces** on the other side. If a player's shot misses the table, hits the net, or they can't return their opponent's shot, the other player or team gets a point. Games are usually played to 11.

Origins

Table tennis was invented in England in the 1800s as an after-dinner game. Today, it's played all over the world and is **China's national sport**.

Liu Guoliang is one of the best table tennis players ever. After retiring as a player, he went on to coach the Chinese national team.

FACT FILE   Type of sport: Racket

Table tennis balls are small and light. Players need superfast reflexes to return them in time.

Playing with paddles

Players hit the balls with small wooden paddles covered in rubber. One side is designed to add **spin** to the ball, and the other side to add no spin.

Top players hit the ball extremely fast.

China has been the most successful nation at the World Table Tennis Championships, winning 145 gold medals.

Table tennis is the world's most popular racket sport.

 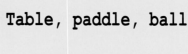

Archery

Archery is the art of using a **bow** to shoot **arrows** at a **target**. The closer an archer gets their arrows to the center of the target, the more points they score.

An ancient art

People have been using bows and arrows for thousands of years. They were originally used for **hunting**, then became a battle weapon before guns and cannons were invented.

During the Middle Ages, archers could shoot between 10-12 arrows a minute.

FACT FILE   Type of sport: Target

Olympic archery

Archery became an Olympic sport in **1900** but wasn't a permanent one until 1972. **South Korea** has been the most successful nation, picking up 23 gold medals over the years.

South Korea's Kim Soo-Nyung is the most successful archer in Olympic history. She has won four gold medals.

← Arrow

The type of bow used at the Olympics is called a "recurve bow." It's based on a design that is 3,500 years old!

← Arm guard

Recurve bow →

Hitting the target

Archers aim their arrows at a target with **10 rings**. Hitting the center circle—the "**bull's-eye**" is worth **10 points**. Every ring farther away from the bull's-eye is worth **one less point**.

Number of players:

1

Equipment: Bow and arrows

Darts

The first darts were arrows that had been cut down.

Darts is a sport where players score points by throwing small **arrows**, called "darts," at a round **target**.

How to play

Players start with a score of 301 or 501 and try to reach **exactly zero**. They take turns throwing three darts, adding up the score, and subtracting it from their total. Players must finish on a "double" or the "inner bull's-eye."

The board

A dartboard is a round target made of different sections numbered from one to 20. Each section also has a **double** and **triple** ring worth double or triple points, an **outer bull's-eye** (worth 25 points), and an **inner bull's-eye** (worth 50).

Quick math

Darts players need to be accurate, but they also need to be good at **math**. If they make a mistake, they need to quickly work out a new way to get to zero in the fewest possible throws.

England's Phil Taylor is the greatest darts player of all time. His nickname is "The Power."

FACT FILE   Type of sport: Target

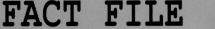

180!

The highest score a player can achieve in a single turn is 180. To do this they must throw all three darts into the triple 20 ring, which gives:

60 + 60 + 60 = 180!

Outer bull's-eye

Double

301-180=???

Inner bull's-eye

Triple

Extreme sports

These sports are for people who **live life on the edge**! They involve risk, speed, height, a battle against Mother Nature, or all of the above!

Parkour

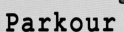

Developed in France in the 1980s, parkour is also known as free-running. The aim is to move over and through obstacles by running, jumping, and climbing.

BMX

Cyclists on BMX bikes race around a dirt track with bumps, ramps, and sharp turns. BMX stands for "bicycle motocross."

White-water rafting

White-water rafters go down a river's fast-moving rapids in an inflatable raft.

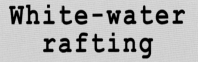

BASE jumping

BASE jumping is similar to skydiving, except people leap from high objects, such as buildings or cliffs, instead of out of a plane.

Skydiving

Skydivers leap out of a plane and then freefall before opening their parachutes to land gently on the ground.

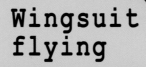

Wingsuit flying

Wingsuit fliers jump out of planes and use special winged suits to glide through the air before parachuting to the ground.

Parasailing

Parasailers are towed behind a fast boat while strapped to a parasail, which lifts up and flies above the water.

Canyoning

Canyoning is a way of exploring canyons by walking, scrambling, climbing, jumping, and swimming.

Slacklining

This is a sport where people walk on a rope between two points. The rope is usually high above the ground.

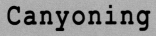

Bungee jumping

Bungee jumpers jump from a great height with an elastic rope attached to their ankles; the rope springs them back up.

Mountaineering

Mountaineering, or **alpinism**, is the name for climbing mountains, but it also involves other types of climbing, both indoor and out.

Race to the top

People have always climbed mountains, but in 1760, Swiss scientist and climber Horace-Bénédict de Saussure made news by offering a reward to anyone who could climb Mount Blanc in France. Then, in 1854, English mountaineer Sir Alfred Wills founded the first climbing club, helping start **"The Golden Age of Alpinism."**

Clamps

Sir Alfred Wills

All the gear

Equipment varies based on **conditions**. In snow and ice, climbers wear **crampons** (a special spiked boot) and use an ice pick for **grip**. In rocky conditions, they hammer **clamps** into the rock, which they attach ropes to, and wear smooth shoes for grip.

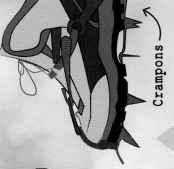

Crampons

Ice pick

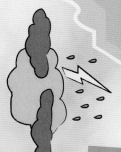

Dangers

Mountaineers face many dangers when climbing peaks, including **rock falls**, **ice falls**, **avalanches**, and **crevasses**. But a change in the **weather** is sometimes the greatest threat. At heights, weather can change quickly, leaving climbers stranded.

Climbers usually work in pairs and are roped together, with one "belaying" the other to catch them if they fall.

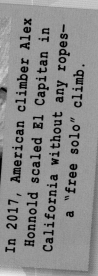

In 2017, American climber Alex Honnold scaled El Capitan in California without any ropes—a "free solo" climb.

FACT FILE

Type of sport: Extreme

Number of players: 1+

Equipment: Rope, clamps, picks, boots, helmet

Skateboarding

Skateboarders ride a **board with wheels** to do tricks and jumps. Skateboarding's first appearance at the Olympics was in Tokyo, Japan, in 2020.

The first skateboard competition was held in California in 1963.

Sidewalk surfing

Skateboarding was invented by American **surfers** who were looking for something fun to do when the **ocean was calm**. They attached wheels to a short surfboard, and a new sport was born. It was originally called "sidewalk surfing."

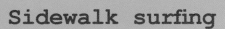

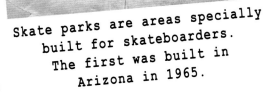

Skate parks are areas specially built for skateboarders. The first was built in Arizona in 1965.

FACT FILE　　Type of sport:　　　Extreme

Tricky!

There are lots of tricks to learn, but the "**ollie**" is the most important. This is where the rider and board leap into the air. It is one of the first tricks a skateboarder must master.

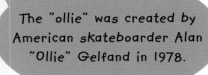

The "ollie" was created by American skateboarder Alan "Ollie" Gelfand in 1978.

Before skate parks were invented, skateboarders used to practice in empty SWIMMING POOLS!

American Tony Hawk is the most successful skateboarder in history. He is famous for a trick called the "900," which is two-and-a-half full turns in the air.

Snooker

Snooker is played on a big table using a stick called a **cue** and a set of balls. The goal is to knock the "cue ball" into other balls so they fall into the table's pockets.

Potting

Knocking the balls into the pockets is called "**potting**" them. Each colored ball earns a different number of points when potted.

Pocket

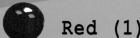 Red (1)

Yellow (2)

Green (3)

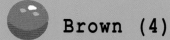 Brown (4)

Blue (5)

Pink (6)

Black (7)

Early snooker balls were made from animal bones or tusks.

The balls must be potted in a special order: a red, then a color, then a red, then a color. The colored balls are replaced each time until all 15 red balls are potted.

When all 15 red balls have been potted, the player pots the yellow, green, brown, blue, pink, and black balls in that order.

Players keep going until they miss a pot. The winner is the player with the most points at the end of the game.

FACT FILE   Type of sport: Stick and ball

Players add chalk to the tips of their cues to help add spin to their shots.

Cue ball

Pool

Pool is a similar sport played on a smaller table, but with fewer balls. There are different versions, but in most, players sink their balls in any order, then end with the black.

Big break

Potting multiple balls in a row is called a **break**. A maximum break happens if a player pots all 15 red balls, followed by 15 blacks, and then all the other colors. This gives them a total score of **147**.

The word "snooker" comes from the word for an inexperienced soldier.

| Number of players: | 2 | Equipment: | 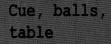 Cue, balls, table |

Bowling

Rolling a ball is simple, but bowling is much harder! There are two main types of bowling: **lawn bowls** and **tenpin**.

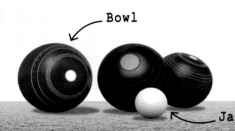

Bowl

Jack

Lawn bowls

The goal of lawn bowls is to roll a ball so it stops as close as possible to a smaller ball called a "**jack**." It's played on grass.

The balls used in lawn bowls are not perfectly round. This means skilled players can curve the ball when they bowl it.

Similar versions of **LAWN BOWLS** called **BOULES**, **RAFFA**,

Tenpin

In tenpin bowling, a player bowls a ball down a **wooden lane**. The goal is to knock down as many of the 10 pins as possible.

Bowling ball

Gutters

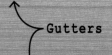

94 **FACT FILE**   Type of sport: Ball

Scoring

The player whose ball is closest to the jack when all balls have been played **wins a point**. If a player has two balls closest, they get two points. The first player to reach 21 points wins.

> Long ago in England, bowls was banned because the King thought it would distract soldiers from practicing their archery!

BOCCE, and **PÉTANQUE** are played around the world.

If a player knocks down all 10 pins in one attempt, it's called a "strike."

> Three strikes in a row are called a "TURKEY!"

How to play

Bowlers have two attempts to knock down all 10 pins. The bowling lane has "gutters" down each side that collect badly bowled balls.

Pins →

Tenpin bowling is the most played sport in the US.

Number of players: 2-6

Equipment:  Bowls and jack or bowling ball and pins

Golf

Golf is a sport where players use clubs to hit a ball into a hole. The goal is to get around a golf course in the **fewest** number of shots.

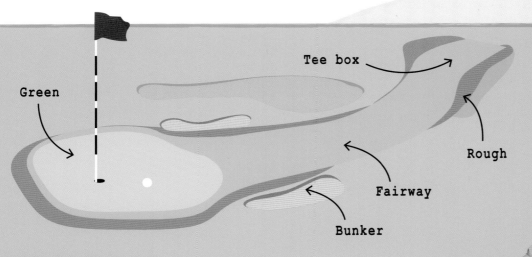

Green

Tee box

Rough

Fairway

Bunker

The course

A golf course is usually made of 9 or 18 holes. For each hole, the player starts on a **tee box**, hits the ball down the **fairway**, trying to avoid the **rough** (long grass) and **bunkers** (sand traps). Once they are on the **green**, the player tries to putt the ball into the **hole**.

FACT FILE   Type of sport:    Stick and ball

Astronauts have even played golf on the MOON!

Wood

Iron

Putter

Different clubs

Golfers use different types of club for different shots. **Woods** help players hit the ball a long way, **irons** are used for more precise shots, and a **putter** is used to tap the ball into the hole.

Every hole has a "par" number, which is the number of shots you are expected to take to get the ball in the hole. The more shots under par you get, the better.

-4	Condor	Four shots better than par
-3	Double Eagle (Albatross)	Three shots better than par
-2	Eagle	Two shots better than par
-1	Birdie	One shot better than par
0	Par	The expected number of shots
+1	Bogey	One shot worse than par
+2	Double bogey	Two shots worse than par
+3	Triple bogey	Three shots worse than par

The first golf balls were stuffed with goose feathers and were known as "featheries."

Putt-putt golf

Mini golf is a fun version of golf played on a tiny course using only a putter. Players have to avoid obstacles and make trick shots.

Windmill obstacle

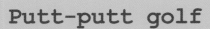

Unusual sports

Some sports around the world sound too weird or silly to be true, but, believe it or not, these are real sports...

Chess boxing

Chess boxing is exactly what it sounds like— rounds of chess and rounds of boxing! Players win by getting checkmate in chess or knocking out an opponent in boxing.

Extreme ironing

The goal is to iron clothes in extreme conditions, such as while skydiving, underwater, or in a snowstorm!

Toe wrestling

Toe wrestling is a little like arm wrestling. Competitors lock their big toes and try to pin down their opponent's foot.

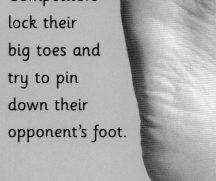

Cheese rolling

Players chase a wheel of cheese down a hill and try to catch up with it. Usually they just fall over though!

Shin kicking

Two opponents line up against each other, grab one another by the collar, and actually kick each other in the shins!

Octopush

Also called underwater hockey, octopush involves players moving a puck across a pool floor into their opponent's goal.

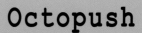

Bog snorkeling

Competitors try to swim two lengths of a muddy ditch as fast as possible.

Egg throwing

The goal in egg throwing is to throw and catch eggs from the farthest distance possible without breaking them. It's harder than it sounds!

Fjerljeppen

This sport comes from the Netherlands. It means "far leaping." People shimmy up a pole as it is falling and try to land on the other side of a canal.

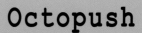

Ice hockey

Sliding
sports

Ski jumping

Biathlon

Skiing

Figure
skating

Winter sports

When summer is over, there are lots of sports to play on the **ice and snow**. All of these sports are part of the Winter Olympics, which happens every four years. Wrap up warm and take a look at these chilly sports.

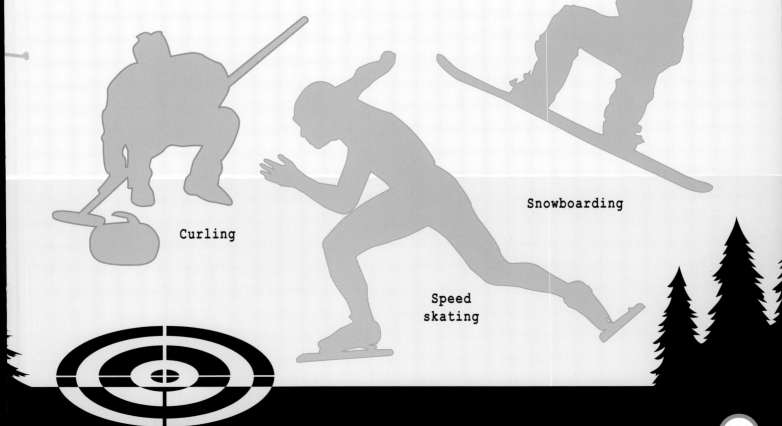

Curling

Speed skating

Snowboarding

Skiing

Skiers have been gliding over snow for fun, and to get around, for thousands of years. Skiing became popular as a sport in the 18th century, and there are now two types: **alpine** and **Nordic**.

Alpine

In alpine skiing, skiers glide **down hills**. There are **four events**: downhill, slalom, giant slalom, and super giant slalom (Super G).

Downhill is all about speed. Skiers start near the top of a mountain and rush down a steep, twisty course as quickly as possible.

Slalom is a shorter race for master turners. Skiers make short, quick turns between poles or gates.

Giant slalom skiers race over a longer course between a series of gates. The gates are spaced farther apart than in slalom races.

Super G combines the speed of downhill with the precision skiing of giant slalom.

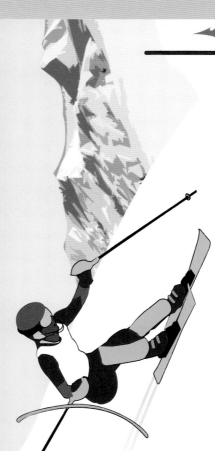

Downhill skiers reach speeds of up to **80MPH (130KPH)**.

In Nordic skiing, only the toe of the boot is attached to the ski, so skiers can lift their heels while skiing.

Nordic

Nordic skiing includes **cross-country skiing** and **Telemark skiing**. Cross-country ski races take place over long distances and require great **stamina**. Telemark skiing requires a mix of skills from both alpine skiing and Nordic skiing.

Marcel Hirscher

Masters of the piste

Austria has been skiing's most successful country at the Winter Olympic Games. Austrian Marcel Hirscher is one of the **best alpine skiers ever**.

FACT FILE

Type of sport: Winter

Number of players: 1

Equipment: Skis, poles, boots, helmet, goggles, gloves

Ski jumping

Ski jumping is a sport where skiers speed down a ramp, launch through the air, and try to jump as **far as they can**.

Ski jumpers can reach speeds of **65MPH (105kph)** on the biggest hills.

Taking flight

When ski jumpers launch from the ramp, they can glide through the air for around 10 seconds and travel as far as **two soccer fields**!

Jumping ramp

Takeoff table

Ski jumping started in Norway more than 100 years ago.

Sondre Norheim came up with the idea to fully strap his boots to skis rather than just the toe. He used his invention to win the first ski jumping competition, held in Høydalsmo, Norway, in 1866.

FACT FILE

Type of sport: Winter

High on the hill

Ski jumping venues are called **hills**. Hills are made up of a **jumping ramp**, **takeoff table**, and **landing hill**.

Ski jumpers hold their skis in a V-shape when flying through the air to help them jump farther.

Ski jumping has been an Olympic sport since 1924.

Austrian Stefan Kraft holds the world record for the longest ski jump at 832ft (253.5m)

Landing hill

Number of players: **1**

Equipment:  Skis, boots, helmet, goggles, gloves

Biathlon

Biathlon is a winter endurance sport that combines cross-country **skiing** and rifle **shooting**. The biathlete who records the fastest time wins.

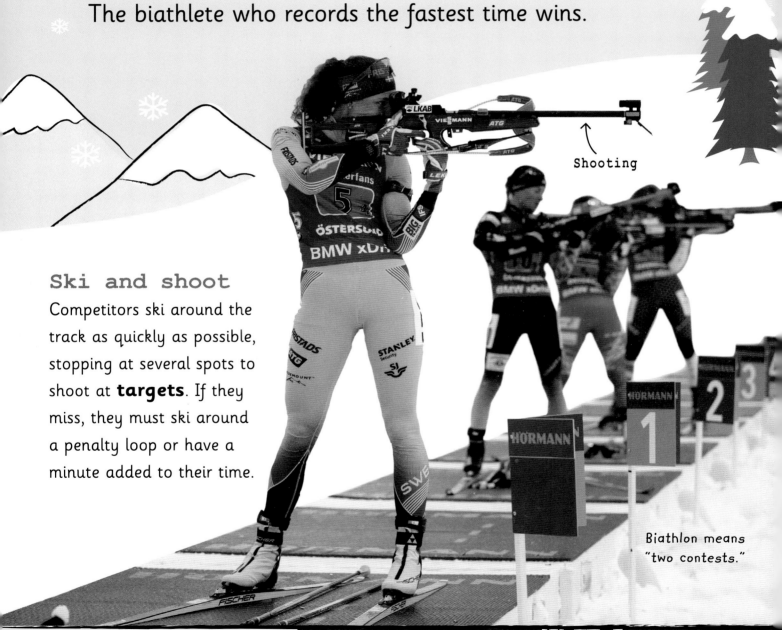

Shooting

Ski and shoot

Competitors ski around the track as quickly as possible, stopping at several spots to shoot at **targets**. If they miss, they must ski around a penalty loop or have a minute added to their time.

Biathlon means "two contests."

FACT FILE   Type of sport

King of Biathlon

Norway's Ole Einar Bjørndalen is one of the **greatest** biathletes ever. Ole won 13 medals at the Winter Olympics, 8 of them gold.

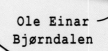

Ole Einar Bjørndalen

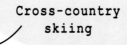

Cross-country skiing

Target

Superhuman shooting

Shooting a rifle always takes skill, but it's especially tricky during a biathlon. Cross-country skiing is tiring, so when an athletes stops to shoot, their heart is pounding, making it very hard to hold a rifle steady.

Biathletes carry their rifles on their backs as they ski.

Biathlon goes back 2,000 years, when Scandinavian hunters set off skiing with a weapon over their shoulders.

Snowboarding

The sport of snowboarding was inspired by **skateboarding**, **surfing**, and **skiing**. A snowboarder glides down slopes on a long board.

Snowboard styles

From **racing** and performing **tricks**, to **jumping** as high as possible, boarders have lots of ways to enjoy the snow.

Jibbing
This is a technique where a boarder rides and performs tricks on surfaces such as rails, benches, logs, and rocks.

Freeriding
This is snowboarding on an open mountainside. There are no rules to follow and no set course.

Slopestyle
Snowboarders perform tricks while riding down a course packed with obstacles such as jumps, boxes, or rails.

Racing
Snowboarders race down a course similar to a giant slalom course used in skiing. Riders have to pass through a series of gates.

Big air
Riders perform tricks after launching themselves off a big ramp.

Snowboarding became a Winter Olympic sport at the 1998 Games in Nagano, Japan.

Snurfing

Although it developed in several places, the origins of snowboarding go back to 1965, when American engineer **Sherman Poppen** strapped two skis together so his daughters could have more control while skiing. He called the invention a "**snurfer**" and the idea caught on!

Half-pipe

Boardercross

Several riders race down a special course. The first to cross the finish line wins the race.

Alpine snowboarding

This is when snowboarders ride on the runs used by skiers. It's fast and full of skillful turns.

Half-pipe

Riders perform tricks while riding along a huge, semicircular tube.

Number of players: 1

Equipment: Snowboard, helmet, goggles, gloves

Speed skating

There are two types of speed skating: long track and short track. Both have the same goal—race around an ice track as **fast as possible**!

Short track racing was invented in the US where there were plenty of ice rinks.

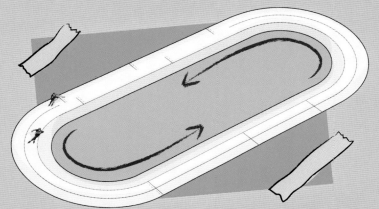

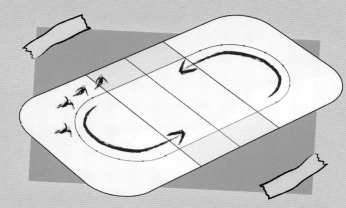

Long track races are held on a large oval. Only two skaters race at one time. Races can be between 500m and 10,000m. The first to finish is the winner.

Short track races take place on ice rinks. The skaters all race at once but must not get in each others' way; they are disqualified if they do. Races are between 500m and 5,000m.

Speed skaters look like they glide effortlessly on the ice, but they're moving at fast speeds!

FACT FILE   Type of sport: Winter

South Korean flag

Korean dominance

Since short-track speed skating became an Olympic event in 1992, **South Korean** skaters have dominated, winning 48 medals, including 24 golds.

With a record 11 Olympic medals, Ireen Wüst of the Netherlands is the most successful long track speed skater ever.

Ireen Wüst

Steady skating

As with all sports, speed skating success can be about **luck**! In the 2002 Olympics, Australia's Steven Bradbury was in last place, but all of his opponents fell over. He stayed on his skates, crossed the finish line first, and won gold.

Skaters always race in a COUNTER-CLOCKWISE direction.

Steven Bradbury

Figure skating

Figure skating is a sport where individuals or pairs perform rehearsed **dance routines** on ice while wearing **skates**.

Skating's start

The sport of figure skating is credited to Americans **Edward Bushell**, who introduced the ice skates that allowed skaters to jump and turn, and **Jackson Haines**, a ballet master who added dance elements.

Jackson Haines

Routines

Skaters perform **dances** called **programs**, which must include spins, jumps, and throws (if dancing in pairs). Judges award points based on how difficult the routine is.

112   **FACT FILE**   Type of sport: Winter

Ice skating existed long before the sport. As early as the 13th century, the Dutch used ice skates to travel around on frozen canals.

The triple axel is one of the most difficult jumps.

Jumps

Skaters perform jumps with different names such as the **toe loop**, **trip**, **lutz**, **salchow**, and **axel**. Skaters use diffferent parts of the blade on their skates to perform these jumps.

Sonja Henie

Figure skating has produced some world-famous stars, such as Norway's Sonja Henie. She made her Olympic debut at 11 years old and later became a Hollywood movie star.

Figure skaters must be strong, agile, and ACROBATIC.

Number of players: 1-2

Equipment: Ice skates

Ice hockey

Ice hockey is similar to field hockey, but instead of being played on grass, it's played on **ice** with **skates** strapped on.

Out on the rink

Ice hockey players wear skates and move around an ice court called a **rink**. Instead of a ball, they hit a small disk called a **puck**.

Staying safe

With sharp skates, flying pucks, big sticks, and fast, strong players whizzing around, players need to wear **pads**. The **goalkeeper** has the most dangerous job, so is covered head to toe in **protective clothing**.

Puck

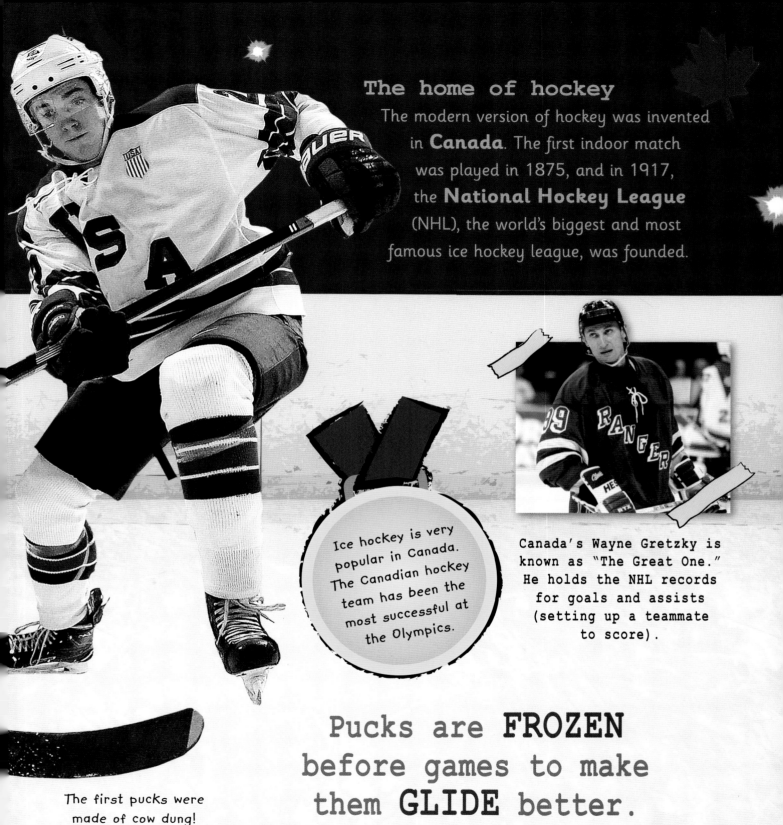

The home of hockey

The modern version of hockey was invented in **Canada**. The first indoor match was played in 1875, and in 1917, the **National Hockey League** (NHL), the world's biggest and most famous ice hockey league, was founded.

Ice hockey is very popular in Canada. The Canadian hockey team has been the most successful at the Olympics.

Canada's Wayne Gretzky is known as "The Great One." He holds the NHL records for goals and assists (setting up a teammate to score).

The first pucks were made of cow dung!

Pucks are **FROZEN** before games to make them **GLIDE** better.

Players per team: 6

Equipment:  Puck, skates, helmet, hockey stick, and pads

Sliding sports

Sliding sports are winter sports where people slide over **ice** with **sleds**. Some sliding sports are high-speed time trials on a **special track**, while others are long-distance races over frozen land.

> Bobsled gets its name from the way riders *bob* back and forth in the sled to make it go faster.

Bobsled

Bobsled

Bobsled is a winter sport where teams of **two** or **four** riders speed down a **twisty track**. The goal is to go as fast as possible!

> Bobsled tracks are made of concrete, then coated with ice. There are only 16 tracks in the world used for competitions.

Luge

In the luge, riders **lie on their backs** on a sled and slide **feetfirst** around a bobsled track. Like bobsled, the aim is to record the fastest time possible.

Germany has dominated the luge at the Winter Olympics.

Skeleton

Luge

Skeleton

Skeleton is a high-speed sliding sport in which riders race **headfirst** down a bobsled track. They lie on their **front** on a small sled.

Skeleton riders can reach speeds of 80mph (130kph)!

Sled dog racing

This sport is particularly popular in the world's **Arctic regions**—Russia, Greenland, and North America. A team of **dogs** pulls a **sled** and **rider** (musher). Teams race over courses, and the fastest team wins.

Curling

In curling, teams slide big **stones** along a slippery sheet of ice and try to get them to stop on a target called the **house**. The closer they get to the middle of the house, the better.

Players can use their stones to knock the other team's stones away from the target to keep them from scoring.

Curling stone

House

At the Olympics

Curling was first played at the Winter Olympics in Calgary, Canada, in 1998. **Canada** has been the most successful nation, winning three golds in the men's event and two golds in the women's event.

FACT FILE   Type of sport: Winter

Skillful sliding

Sliding the stone to exactly where you want can be tricky on the smooth ice. To help it along, "**sweepers**" brush the ice in front of the stone with special brooms. The harder they sweep, the farther the stone travels.

Sweeper

The captain of a curling team is called the "SKIP."

The skip shouts out orders to the rest of the team so that they know where and how hard to sweep the ice with their brooms.

Curling is called the "roaring game" because of the sound the stone makes sliding on the ice.

A very old game

Curling has been played in Scotland, Belgium, and the Netherlands for centuries. The oldest curling stone ever found dates to 1511. It was found in a pond in Scotland.

Players per team: 4

Equipment: Curling stone and brooms

Diving

Kayaking

Water polo

Swimming

Rowing

Water sports

While most sports are played on land, there are plenty that take place on or in the water. Whether they involve swimming or steering a boat, all these sports require **speed**, **power**, **and stamina**. Let's dive in!

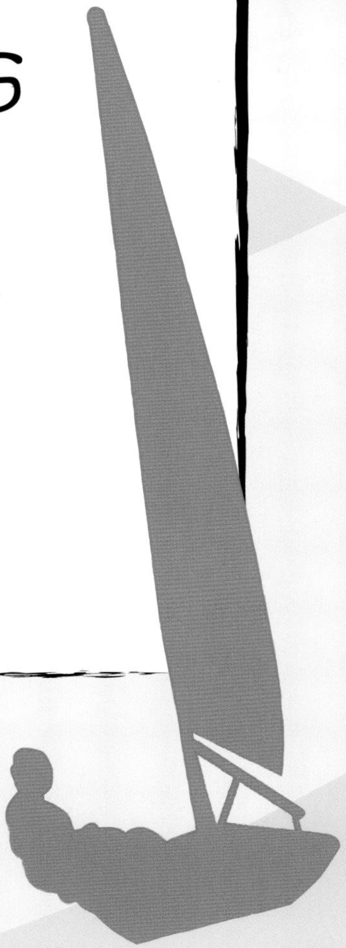

Sailing

Surfing

Swimming

Swimmers use their arms and legs to push themselves through the water. There are four different swimming **strokes**, each with its own technique.

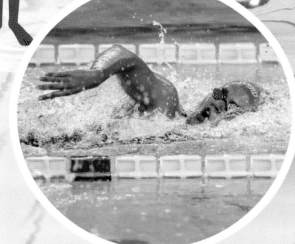

Top swimmers are very muscular and usually have broad shoulders.

Freestyle

Also known as front crawl, this is the fastest stroke. The swimmer moves their arms forward in turn while constantly kicking their feet.

Butterfly

This is the most difficult stroke. The swimmer throws both arms forward, then pulls them back along each side of their body while performing a dolphin kick with their legs.

FACT FILE   Type of sport: Water

Swimming is one of only five sports that have been at every Olympic Games.

Open-water swimming

Swimming in **lakes** or in the **sea** is known as open-water swimming. Open-water swimming is a long race that requires amazing stamina.

Freedivers hold their breath and try to dive as deep as possible. Top freedivers can hold their breath for up to 10 minutes!

The first Olympic swimming competition was held in the sea.

10

Backstroke

The swimmer lies on their back and kicks their legs while lifting one arm over their head and then pulling it through the water. They then repeat with the other arm.

Breaststroke

This is the slowest stroke. The swimmer pushes both arms straight out in front of them, then pulls each arm to their side in a big semicircle. The legs perform a "frog kick."

Number of players: 1-8

Equipment: Swimsuit, goggles, cap

Diving

Diving is the skill of **jumping** into water from a height while performing acrobatic moves.

Types of diving

There are two forms of competitive diving: **platform diving**, which takes place in a pool, and **cliff diving**, where divers leap from a platform into the sea.

Cliff diving

In cliff diving, divers **launch** themselves from a cliff into the sea. No one knows the exact origins, but it's been done for hundreds of years in many parts of the world.

Platform diving

Divers, either **alone** or in **pairs**, leap from platforms into a pool. During the dive, they perform **moves** and are judged on how difficult the dive was and how well they pulled it off.

Diving partners Guo Jingjing and Wu Minxia from China are two of the best divers ever.

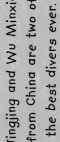

Guo Jingjing

Wu Minxia →

Divers must get into
one of these four
positions
during a dive:

Straight: a diver
is not allowed to
have any bends in
the hips or knees.

Pike: a diver bends
their body but keeps
their legs straight.

Free: a twisted dive
that includes a combination
of the other three dives.

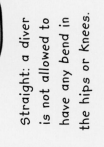

Tuck: a diver tucks
their body into a ball.

There are cliff
diving tournaments all
over the world.

If a diver enters the water
without making a splash,
it is known as a "RIP."

FACT FILE

Type of sport:
Water

Number of
players: 1-2

Equipment:
swimwear

125

Surfing

Surfers, sometimes called "wave riders," stand on surfboards to **catch a wave** and ride it back to shore.

Many surfers have **BOLD**, personal designs on their boards.

The rise of surfing

Surfing has been part of the culture of the Pacific Islands for centuries. Pacific Islanders shared surfing with the world by **teaching tourists** how to catch waves.

Hawaii

Experienced surfers can do tricks as they ride the wave.

To ride a wave, surfers lie on their boards and face the shore. When a good wave comes, they paddle and try to match its speed. Once the wave carries them forward, they stand up and ride it.

FACT FILE   Type of sport: Water

Through the tube

When a surfer rides inside the curl of a breaking wave, it's called a "**tube ride**."

Tube riders try to stand inside the curl without it collapsing on them.

When a surfer comes off their board, it's called a "WIPEOUT."

George Freeth© 1914 - 2014

Hawaiian lifeguard George Freeth is considered one of the fathers of surfing. Raised on the beaches of Hawaii, Freeth was spotted surfing and invited to California to show off his skills and love of surfing.

Number of players: 1

Equipment: Surfboard and wetsuit

Water polo

This sport is a little like handball or rugby, but in water. Two teams **swim around**, passing a ball to each other and shooting at the other team's goal.

Start of a sport

In 1877, Scottish swimming instructor William Wilson came up with a set of rules, and the first water polo match took place on the Dee River in **Scotland**. After that, the sport became popular in the UK and around the world.

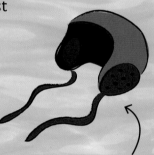

Ear guards are used for protection, but also help identify who is on each team.

Ear guards

anti

Goalkeeper

Playing the game

Unlike with most team sports, water polo players don't really stay in any set **positions** (other than the goalkeeper). The players can move around the pool according to the situation.

FACT FILE   Type of sport: Water

Players can only hold the ball in ONE HAND.

Contact sport

Players are allowed to grab each others' arms and legs, but most games are clean. The 1956 Olympic game between Hungary and the USSR, however, was **so rough** that players were injured—it is known as the "Blood in the Water" match. The Soviets had recently crushed a Hungarian uprising against the USSR.

Players use a technique known as an "eggbeater kick" to stay upright as they play. It's called this because the motion of the player's legs is like the motion cooks make when they whisk eggs.

Eggbeater kick

Players per team: 7

Equipment: Swimwear, mouth guard, ear guards, ball

Kayaking

Kayaking is a water sport where people move a **small boat** through water using a special paddle.

Kayaking can be slow and relaxing in calm waters or exhilarating in dangerously fast rapids.

The LONGER a kayak is...

Early transportation

Kayaks were invented by the Inuit people from North America. They were originally used for hunting and fishing. The word kayak means "**hunter's boat**."

FACT FILE   Type of sport:    Water

White-water kayaking

In 1931, Germany's Adolf Anderle kayaked down the **rushing waters** of the Salzachöfen Gorge in Austria. This is thought to be the birth of white-water kayaking, which gets its name because rushing water rapids look white.

...the FASTER it goes.

In 1928, Germany's Franz Romer kayaked across the Atlantic Ocean. It took him 58 days!

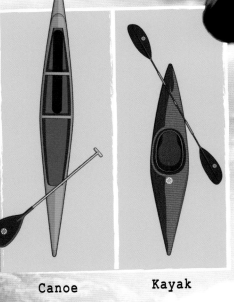

Canoe   Kayak

Kayak or canoe?
A lot of people mix up kayaks with canoes, but a good way to tell the difference is to remember kayakers sit **inside the boat**, and canoes have a raised seat. They also use different paddles.

Number of players: 1-4

Equipment: Kayak, paddle, helmet, life jacket

131

Rowing

Rowers use **oars** to move their **boat** through water. They race each other one-on-one, or in teams of up to eight rowers and a **cox**, who steers and coordinates the other members of the team.

Up the river

Rowing has been a good way to move on water since ancient times. For centuries, ferrymen in London, England, took passengers up and down the **Thames River**, and eventually started racing to see who was fastest.

Every year since 1829, rowers from Oxford and Cambridge Universities row against each other in a famous race.

FACT FILE   Type of sport: Water

At the first modern Olympics in 1896, the rowing competition had to be canceled due to stormy weather!

British rower Steve Redgrave won gold at every Olympic Games between 1984 and 2000.

Cox

Rowers face backward so they can pull their oars and move the boat. This means they can't see where they're going. Only the cox faces forward.

Number of players: 1-9

Equipment: Rowing boat, oars

Sailing

Sailboats use the power of the **wind** to move over **water**.

Sailing is one of the world's oldest forms of transportation, but it's also a popular sport.

← Buoy

Sailing as a sport

There are lots of **different types** of sailing **races**, but the boats in each one are usually a similar size and type. The amount of people sailing a boat (the crew) can be as few as one, or up to 15.

Fleet racing

Boats receive points for where they finish in a race. The winner is the boat with the best score after all the races are finished.

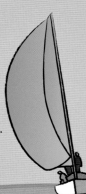

Match racing

Two boats race against each other, and the first boat to cross the finish line wins. The world's most famous sailing race, the America's Cup, is a match race.

Team racing

This is a tactical race in which a team of three boats takes on another team of three boats. The team with the best overall score wins the race.

Sails

Boom

Laura Dekker from the Netherlands sailed around the world by herself when she just 16 years old.

Speed sailing

In speed sailing, boats compete individually and try to go as fast as possible.

Rudder

Parts of a boat

There are many types of boats, and they can look very different from each other. But they all have **sails**, to catch the wind, a **boom**, to control the angle of the sails, and a **rudder**, to steer.

Number of players: 1–15

Equipment: Boat, life vest

Water sports

Water sports are activities that take place either **in the water** or **on the water**.

Scuba diving

With an oxygen tank, scuba divers can swim underwater without needing to come up for air.

ON THE WATER

Waterskiing

Water-skiers stand on skis and hold a cable attached to a speedboat. The boat drags the skier across the water.

PWC

Riders stand on a motorized personal watercraft (PWC) and power their way across the water. Some riders race against each other.

Kite-surfing

Kite-surfers stand on a board and use a kite to pull them across the surface of the water.

IN THE WATER

Snorkeling

Snorkelers use a mask and a pipe called a snorkel to help them breathe while their faces are underwater.

Synchronized swimming

Swimmers perform rehearsed moves together in a pool. The goal is to do the same move at the exact same time.

Wakeboarding

This is similar to water-skiing, but wakeboarders use a board instead of skis.

Windsurfing

Windsurfers ride a board that has a sail attached to it. The wind's power moves surfers through the water.

Dragon boat racing

A team of paddlers moves a long, canoelike boat through the water, often racing against other boats. Teams can be as large as 20 paddlers.

Go

Playground
games

Dodgeball

Tug-of-war

Games

What's more fun than a game? Some games are so simple they can be played by anyone and have no special equipment. Some require strength, some require agility, and then there are board games that call for brains and planning. Which is your **favorite**?

Ultimate

Chess

Ancient games

People have been playing board games for a long, long time. Some of these ancient games are around **5,000 years old**!

Latrunculi

Also known as Mercenaries, this Roman strategy game was played on a board with a grid similar to chess or checkers.

Mehen

No one knows how this ancient Egyptian board game was played, but the board itself was shaped like a snake!

Mehen board

Mancala

Mancala is still played today, but some people think a version of it was played in ancient Egyptian times.

Patolli

Patolli

This game was popular in the Aztec Empire. Players threw stones or beans to decide how their pieces would move around a cross-shaped board.

Petteia

The ancient Greek game of petteia (robbers) was a little like the modern game of checkers. The aim is to capture all of your opponent's pieces.

Senet

This ancient Egyptian board game dates to around 3,100BCE! The word senet means "the game of pulling," but no one knows exactly how it was played.

Terni Lapilli

This game, played in the Roman Empire, was similar to the modern-day game of tic-tac-toe.

The Royal Game of Ur

This strategy game is also known as "The Game of 20 Squares." It was first played around 3,000 BCE in Mesopotamia (ancient Iraq).

Playground games

Playing games is a **fun** way to make friends, but on top of that, games can teach you important skills such as **teamwork** and **coordination**.

Catch the dragon's tail

In this Chinese game, players line up with their hands on the shoulders of the person in front of them. The first person is the dragon's head and the person at the back is the tail. The "head" tries to catch the "tail" while the players in the middle stiffen and try to stop them.

Dan chhae jul normgi

In this traditional Korean game, two players swing a jump rope while other players take turns trying to jump on the rope and stop it from moving. If they succeed, they become a rope holder, but if the rope catches their leg, they are out. The winner is the last player left.

Hide and seek

The rules of hide and seek are simple. The seeker covers their eyes and counts while everyone else hides. Then the seeker has to find them. The last person to be found is the winner.

Rock, paper, scissors

Two players count to three, then use their hands to make the shape of either a rock (a fist), a piece of paper (a flat hand), or a pair of scissors (a V-shape). Rock beats scissors; paper beats rock; and scissors beats paper.

Forty forty

One player is "it" and must guard a "base," such as a tree. The other players run off and hide, then have to get back to the base without being tagged by the guard.

Ten ten

Ten ten is a popular clapping game from Nigeria. In the game, children face each other and clap their hands and move their legs to a rhythm.

Red Rover

Two teams line up and form chains by holding hands. The first team calls out: "Red rover, red rover, send (player's name) right over." The player runs into the other team and tries to break the chain. If they do, they take a player to their team. If not, they join their opponents in the chain. By the end, one team has all the players.

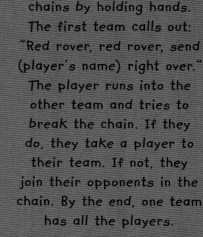

More playground games

Here are some other playground games you can try. Some of these games are played **all around the world**, but will have different names.

It/Tag

This is the simplest of playground games. One person is "it" and must try to tag another player. If they tag another person, that person becomes the new "it," and the game continues.

YOU'RE "IT"

Cat's cradle

This ancient game involves two or more players and a piece of string. Players twist the string into a special shape with their fingers and take turns making shapes with the string.

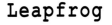

Leapfrog

One player bends over or crouches while another vaults over them. That player then bends over and lets the other player vault over them.

I like to invent my own games!

Double Dutch

This is a jump-rope game that uses two long jump ropes. The ropes are swung in opposite directions while two or more players jump in the middle.

Duck, duck, goose

All players sit in a circle, except one, who walks around the circle, tapping people's heads and saying whether they are a "duck" or a "goose." If someone is a goose, they have to get up and try to tag the person who tagged them before they can sit down in the goose's spot. If the goose can't do this, they become the person outside the circle.

Statues

This game is popular in Greece. Someone is chosen to be "it," closes their eyes and shouts "agalmata!" (which means "statue" in Greek). The other players have to freeze in the shape of famous statues and try not to move.

Capture the flag

Two teams place a flag in a special "base." The goal is to try to steal the other team's flag and return it to your base while also protecting your own flag and keep from being tagged. If players are tagged, they are stuck in "jail" and have to remain still until they are freed by one of their teammates.

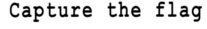

Kongki noli

A traditional Korean game, Kongki noli involves players scattering five stones on the ground, throwing one into the air while picking up another. With each new round of the game, the player has to pick up more and more stones at once.

Tug-of-war

Tug-of-war was part of the Olympics between 1900 and 1920, but has not been included since.

Also known as rope-pulling, tug-of-war is a **test of strength**.
Two teams pull on opposite ends of a rope to try to drag the other team to their side of a line.

Ancient origins

No one really knows where tug-of-war originated, but it's definitely **very old**. Ancient Chinese commanders used the sport to train soldiers, and it's likely generals in ancient Greece did the same.

FACT FILE   Type of sport: Team

The phrase TUG-OF-WAR was first used to describe battles. It wasn't a name for this game until much later.

The middle of the rope is marked to show when one team has successfully pulled the other to their side.

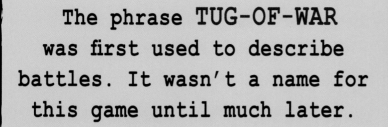

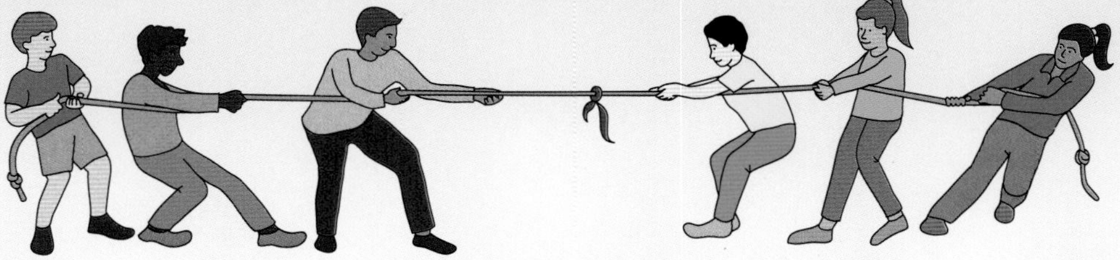

A tug-of-war rope needs to be thick, so it doesn't **SNAP!**

Center line

Players per team: 1-8

Equipment: Rope

Ultimate

In the game of ultimate, players throw a **flying disk** to their teammates while the other team tries to get it from them.

Ultimate origins

Ultimate was invented by a group of American **schoolchildren** in 1968. The sport's first real rules were decided in 1970, and it has grown ever since.

Catching the disk by clapping your hands together is called a **PANCAKE**!

A popular brand of flying disk gets its name from a pie pan, which was made by the Frisbie Pie Company.

FACT FILE   Type of sport: Throwing

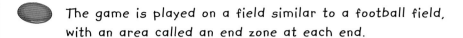

Basic rules

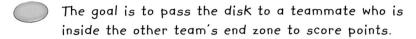

The game is played on a field similar to a football field, with an area called an end zone at each end.

The goal is to pass the disk to a teammate who is inside the other team's end zone to score points.

Players can pass the disk in any direction, but are not allowed to run with it. If an opponent catches a thrown disk, their team gets to keep it.

If the disk doesn't reach a teammate, is dropped, or goes out of the field of play, the other team gets it.

Players are not allowed to bump into or tackle each other.

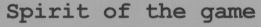

Spirit of the game

Ultimate is one of very few team sports that does not use a **referee**. Instead, the players make all the decisions. This is because everyone who plays is expected to follow the "spirit of the game" and play fairly.

Rock, paper, scissors is sometimes used instead of a coin toss to decide which team starts the game with the disk.

Players per team: 7

Equipment: Flying disk

Dodgeball

Dodgeball is a **fun** team sport where players try to hit their opponents with a ball, while avoiding being hit by balls **thrown** at them by opponents.

How to play

Two teams of six try to get as many of the other team's players out as they can.

- Players throw *balls* at the other team. If the *ball* hits an opponent, they are out; but, if they catch the *ball*, the player who threw it is out.

- Players can *save* a teammate if they catch the *ball* that hit them *before* it touches the ground.

- Players are only allowed to hold the ball for five seconds. If they hold it for longer, they have to give it to the other team.

- If a player steps outside the court or crosses into the other team's half, they are out.

- Games usually last for three minutes. The team with the most players left wins.

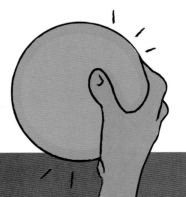

The balls used are usually made of cloth, foam, or rubber, so are soft.

Players are **NOT** allowed to aim at an opponent's **HEAD**.

Dangerous game
The sport is believed to have come from an African game from 200 years ago. Players **threw rocks at each other** to improve **hunting skills** and learn to work as a team.

Players per team: 6

Equipment:  Balls

Chess

Chess is a hugely popular **strategy** game that gets your brain planning moves and thinking ahead. It is played on a checkered board with 64 squares.

Rooks can travel any distance in a straight line.

Pawn   **Rook**   **Knight**

How to win

Each player has **16 pieces**: one king, one queen, two bishops, two knights, two rooks (castles), and eight pawns. The aim is to take your opponent's pieces and **checkmate** your opponent's king by trapping it where it can't move without being taken.

Chessboard

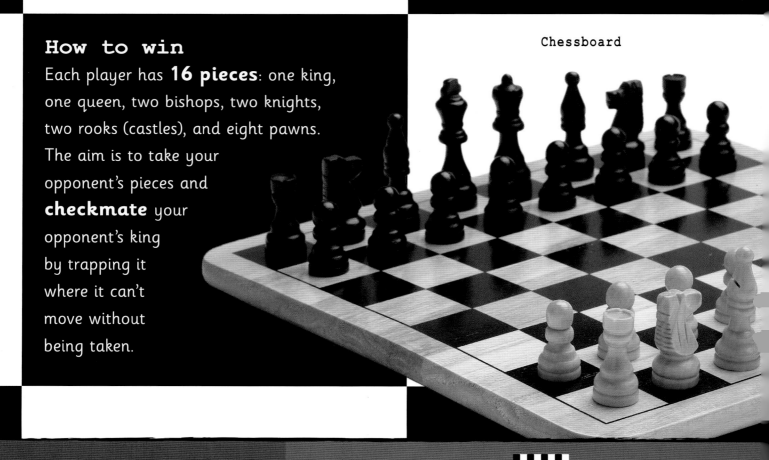

FACT FILE   Type of sport: Board game

Bishop   Queen   King

Bishops can travel any distance, but must move diagonally.

World-class chess champions are called "grandmasters."

In 1886, Wilhelm Steinitz, who was born in modern-day Czech Republic, became the first official chess world champion.

Different directions

Each piece can only move in a certain way. The **queen** is the most powerful piece, because she can move any distance in any direction.

Chess history

Chess is thought to come from the **Indian** game **chaturanga**, which was first played around 1,500 years ago. The official rules used today were decided in the 1880s.

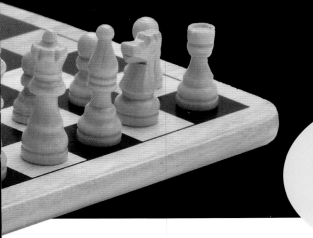

In the Middle Ages, chess was used to teach war strategy.

Number of players: 2

Equipment: Chessboard and pieces

Go

The game of Go is a strategy board game that was invented in China thousands of years ago. It is thought to be the **oldest** board game still played today.

How to play

Players take turns placing their pieces (called "stones") on a board with a grid. One player uses black stones and the other player uses white stones.

Stones can only be placed on empty points of the grid. Once a stone has been placed, it can only be removed when it has been captured by the opponent.

If a stone is surrounded on two sides, either horizontally or vertically, by the opponent's stones, it is "captured" and kept as a "prisoner."

The winner is the player who gains the most captured stones and territory of the board.

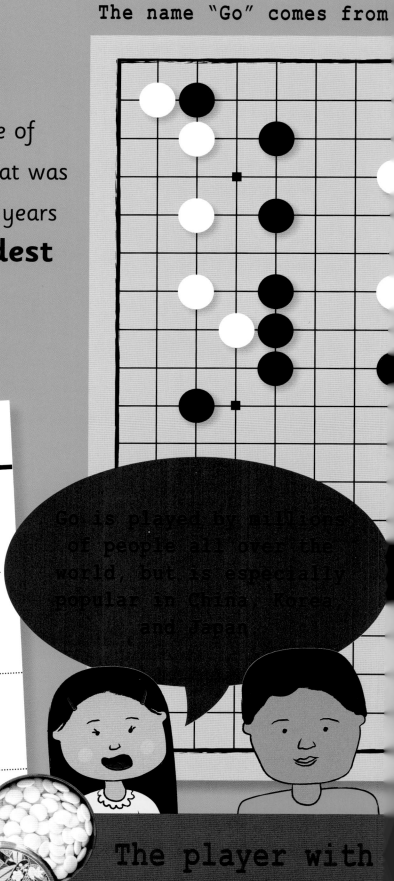

Go is played by millions of people all over the world, but is especially popular in China, Korea, and Japan

The player with

"board game of surrounding."

Gaining territory

The **territory** a player has gained at the end of the game is the number of points on the grid that are surrounded by their stones.

Tactics

Players need to pay attention to which stones can be captured. A major part of Go is the ability to **plan ahead**.

The Ko rule

One of the main rules in Go is called the **Ko rule**. This rule says players are not allowed to make a move that returns the game to its previous position. This stops the game from lasting too long.

In 2016, a computer program using Artificial Intelligence successfully defeated Go master Lee Sedol of Korea.

Sporting stories

All around the world, people look up to athletes because they show us that if we work hard we can do amazing things. From the peak of Mount Everest to the waves of Hawaii, here are some amazing stories about some of the most inspiring moments in **sports history**.

The first marathon

At 26.22 miles (42.2km), the marathon is the **longest** track and field event. Its name comes from a Greek story about a soldier named **Pheidippides**.

Battle news

According to an ancient Greek legend, in **490 BCE**, Pheidippides ran all the way from the battlefield of **Marathon** to Athens, Greece, to let the city know that the Greek army had defeated its enemy. He ran the entire distance of around **25 miles (40km)**.

A marathon was held at the first modern Olympics in Athens in 1896. Greek athlete Spyridon Louis won the race in 2 hours, 58 minutes, 20 seconds.

After delivering the good news to Athens, Pheidippides is said to have died of exhaustion from his long run.

Ethiopia's Abebe Bikila is the only marathon runner to win two gold medals in a row at the Olympics.

Marathons are run all over the world, even in **ANTARCTICA.**

Keep on running!
Spanish athlete **Ricardo Abad** ran an incredible **607 marathons** in **607 days** between October 1, 2010, and February 12, 2012.

Kenya's Eliud Kipchoge broke the 2-hour marathon record with a time of 1 hour, 59 minutes, 40 seconds. Kenya's Brigid Kosgei holds the women's world record with a time of 2 hours, 14 minutes, 4 seconds.

Climbing **Everest**

Reaching 29,029ft (8,848m) into the sky, Mount Everest is the world's tallest mountain. For years, adventurers tried to climb it—but who was **first**?

It takes about 2 months to reach

People who climb Everest need to take oxygen tanks to help them breathe.

Oxygen → mask

Race to the top

In 1856, people figured out that Everest was the world's highest mountain. From then on, the **race was on** to see who could climb it first.

Difficult ascent

Everest is in the Himalayas. It's steep, cold, and so tall there's barely any oxygen near the peak. Many climbers tried and failed to reach the top. One, George Mallory, was once asked why he would attempt such a dangerous climb. He replied, **"Because it's there."**

the peak.

The roof of the world

On May 29, 1953, **Edmund Hillary** and **Tenzing Norgay** were the first people to reach the summit. Since then, more than 7,000 people have followed in their footsteps.

We only spent 15 minutes at the peak before heading back down.

Edmund Hillary was a climber and explorer from New Zealand. He continued adventuring late into his life.

Tenzing Norgay was born near the Himalayas and was a very experienced climber. He founded a company helping others climb Everest.

Sadly, Mount Everest has become covered in litter and crowded, making it even more dangerous.

Japan's Yuichiro Miura (age 80) is the oldest person to reach the summit.

First perfect 10

At the 1976 Olympics in Montréal, Canada, the Romanian gymnast **Nadia Comăneci** stunned the world by receiving the first **perfect score** in Olympic history.

Nadia on the uneven bars

They say that nobody's perfect, but I proved that wrong!

Nobody like Nadia

Nadia was only 14 years old when she competed at the Olympics. She performed her routine on the **uneven bars** event and was incredible. When she finished, the crowd eagerly awaited her score. But something wasn't right—she had only scored 1.0…

After Nadia's performance on the uneven bars, she scored six more perfect tens at the 1976 Olympics. She also won two gold medals at the 1980 Olympics, then retired and moved to the United States in 1989.

Achievements

5 Olympic gold medals
1976—all-around
1976—uneven bars
1976—balance beam
1980—balance beam
1980—floor exercise

2 World Championship gold medals
1978—balance beam
1979—team

Score

1.00

...Getting a perfect score was thought to be impossible, so the scoreboard wasn't built to go up to 10! So instead, it read 1.00.

The crowd was confused at first, but once people realized that 1.00 meant 10.00, the arena erupted in applause!

She was amazing. Why did she only score 1.00?

The four-minute mile

For years, so many athletes had tried and failed to run a mile in **less than four minutes** that most people thought it was physically impossible and couldn't be done.

Roger Bannister

The record breaker

On May 1954, **Roger Bannister**, a medical student at Oxford University, England, finally managed to do it and proved everyone wrong.

Bannister showed that if you work hard you can achieve anything.

Achieving the impossible

On the day of the race, Bannister reached the three-quarter-mile mark in **3 minutes 0.7** seconds. This spurred him on, and, using every bit of energy he had, he managed to stagger over the finish line in **3 minutes, 59.4 seconds**.

There's no such thing as impossible!

Making history

When the results were called out, the announcer said **"3 minutes a—"** but before the sentence ended, the crowd went wild. **History had been made!**

- The four-minute mile has since been broken by more than 1,400 athletes.

- In 1999, Morocco's Hicham El Guerrouj set the world record for the mile, completing it in 3 minutes, 43.13 seconds.

Jesse Owens at the Olympics

At a time when racism was widespread, Jesse Owens proved **Olympic heroes** come from all walks of life, regardless of the color of their skin.

Olympic Stadium

In **1936**, the **Olympic Games** were held in Germany's capital, **Berlin**. Around the same time, Adolf Hitler and the Nazi Party rose to power, so tensions were high.

The 1936 Olympics were the first to be shown **live on TV**. The Nazis wanted to use this event to spread their racist belief that certain groups of white people were better than everyone else.

But America's **Jesse Owens** proved them wrong in a big way. He won **three individual gold medals** in the 100m, 200m, and long jump, and a **fourth** as part of the US men's relay team.

Jesse's heroic performance sent an inspirational message to the rest of the world.

Although it angered the Nazis, most of the **German crowd** found Owens' performance **amazing** and **cheered him on**.

Owens's feat of winning four track and field gold medals didn't happen again until the US's Carl Lewis did it in 1984.

The land speed record

Ever since cars were invented, they've become faster and faster. This means people are constantly competing to see who can drive the **fastest**.

When Andy Green set the record, he went so fast he traveled faster than the speed of sound. This created an explosion called "a sonic boom."

The challenge

People were racing long before the idea of a speed record came about, but the official speed record rules state that a car has to be driven on a **flat course** over 1 mile (previously 1km) in both directions. The time recorded would be the average top speed of **both times**.

Setting the pace

In 1898, Frenchman Gaston de Chasseloup-Laubat, drove an **electric car**, and reached **39.24mph (62.78kph)**. Ever since, people have continued to try and set a new record.

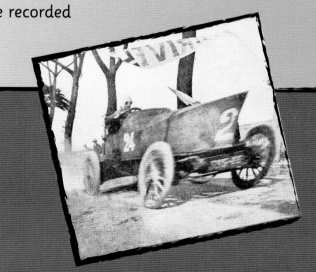

In 1904 France's Louis Rigolly became the first person to drive at more than 100mph.

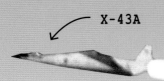

X-43A

The air speed record is a massive 7,310mph (11,764.3Kph) set by the X-43A jet—a plane without a pilot.

The water speed record is held by Australia's Ken Warby. He reached a speed of 317.58mph (511.09kph).

Thrust SSC

The fastest speed on two wheels is **376.363MPH (605.698KPH)** by American **ROCKY ROBINSON**.

In 1927, Britain's Henry Segrave became the first to drive at more than 200mph.

The current record is 763.035mph (1,227.986Kph). It was set in 1997 by Britain's Andy Green in a jet-powered car called Thrust SSC.

Eddie Aikau

Eddie Aikau was a surfer and lifeguard from Hawaii. Although he disappeared at sea, he is still remembered as a **Hawaiian hero** and **surfing legend**.

As a **lifeguard**, Eddie used his surfboard to help people in trouble. He rescued more than 500 people and not a single person drowned on his beach, despite the dangerous waves. Eddie became famous for his brave rescues.

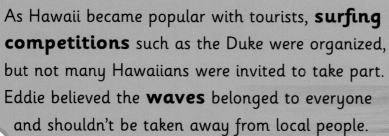

As Hawaii became popular with tourists, **surfing competitions** such as the Duke were organized, but not many Hawaiians were invited to take part. Eddie believed the **waves** belonged to everyone and shouldn't be taken away from local people.

During the Duke competition, he surfed in behind the contestants and impressed everyone so much he was invited to take part the next time. His brother Clyde won in 1973. Eddie **won** in 1977.

Eddie surfed waves that were 40ft (12m) high!

A big-wave competition called "the Eddie" is staged each year in his honor.

Lost at sea

In 1978, Eddie and a crew set off in a canoe on a voyage to Tahiti. The canoe was caught in a storm and started to leak. Eddie paddled out on his board to **find help**.

A few hours later, the canoe was spotted by a plane and the crew was **rescued**. Sadly, Eddie was never seen again.

Eddie's memory lives on today. All across Hawaii, the phrase "Eddie Would Go" is used to describe being willing to take a risk and do the right thing.

Swimming across the **Channel**

The Channel is a 21-mile (36km) wide **stretch of sea** between Britain and France. In 1875, **Matthew Webb** became the first person to successfully swim across it.

Dover

Great Britain

English Channel

France

On August 24, 1875, Englishman Matthew Webb dived into the sea in Dover, England.

More people have reached the top of Mount Everest than have swum the Channel.

In 1926, American **Gertrude Ederle** became the first woman to complete the swim.

Webb headed for France, followed by three small escort boats.

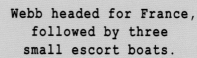

AUGUST
24
1875

On his way he battled strong currents and jellyfish stings, but kept on swimming.

21 hours, 45 minutes later, he arrived exhausted but triumphant in France.

Cap Gris-Nez

Made to swim

Swimming across the Channel was thought to be impossible, but Matthew was no ordinary swimmer. He learned to swim from an early age and spent many years as a **sailor**.

In 2012, Australia's **Trent Grimsey** completed the swim in **6 hours and 55 minutes**.

Britain's **Alison Streeter** has completed the swim an astonishing **46 times**.

Amazing **athletes**

There are good athletes, and then there are the **best of the best**. From breaking records to winning gold medals, these athletes were just built to win. Let's take a look at some of the top athletes of all time in this sporting Hall of Fame.

Serena Williams

Born in 1981, American Serena Williams is one of the most **successful** tennis players ever to grace the court.

A talent for tennis

Serena started playing tennis at the age of **three**. She turned professional at **14** and, four years later, won her first **Grand Slam**. It would not be her last!

A is for ace,
B is for ball,
C is for champion!

The greatest

This was the start of a **stunning career**. By 2019, she had won **23** Grand Slam singles titles, **14** Grand Slam doubles titles, and been the world's top-ranked female player for **319** weeks of her career.

Serena has also won four Olympic gold medals.

Serena's sister Venus is also one of the best players ever. When they teamed up in doubles they were almost unstoppable.

Career highlights

She has won the US Open six times, the Australian Open seven times, the French Open three times, and Wimbledon seven times.

She was ranked world number 1 for 186 weeks in a row.

1

33

She has reached 33 Grand Slam singles finals and won 23 of them.

She played against her sister Venus in nine Grand Slam singles finals. She won seven of them.

9

She is the highest-earning female athlete of all time.

On top of being a tennis legend, she is a successful fashion designer.

Tiger Woods

Born in the US in 1975, Eldrick **"Tiger"** Woods is one of the most famous and successful athletes ever. Not just in golf, but in any sport.

Little tiger

Coached by this father, Tiger started playing golf at the **age of two** and showed huge talent right away. He was so good, he was invited to be on television to show off his golf skills the same year.

The master of Masters

After competing in junior tournaments and turning professional, Tiger became a global superstar in 1997 by winning the **Masters**, one of golf's biggest tournaments, by a record-breaking 12 shots, when he only 21.

The color of power

On the final day of a tournament Tiger always wears a **red shirt**. This is because his mother believes that red is his "power color".

15 He has won 15 major golf titles.

5 He is one of only five players to have won all four of golf's major championships.

81 He has won 81 PGA (Professional Golfer's Association) Tour titles.

1 He was ranked the world's number 1 player for 281 weeks in a row between 2008 and 2010.

20 He has scored 20 hole-in-ones throughout his career.

His success has earned him more than $1 billion!

5 He has won the Masters five times.

Shaun White

Born in California in 1986, Shaun White took up snowboarding when he was **six** years old. He went on to become the most **successful** snowboarder in history.

Triple gold

Shaun won **gold medals** at the 2006 and 2010 Winter Olympics. In 2018, he won gold again, becoming the first snowboarder ever to win **three** gold medals.

White performed so well on his first two runs in 2010 he knew he would win even if he failed his McTwist—but he still wanted to show it to the crowd!

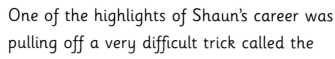
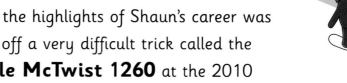

Tricky!

One of the highlights of Shaun's career was pulling off a very difficult trick called the **Double McTwist 1260** at the 2010 Winter Olympics. The trick involves **two flips** and **three and a half spins** at once!

Career highlights

7 TODAY

He won his first snowboard competition at the age of seven.

He became a national champion for the first time in 2003, when he was just 16 years old!

16

3

He is the first snowboarder in history to win three Olympic golds.

13

He holds the record for snowboarding gold medals at the X Games tournament, with 13.

He is also a professional skateboarder.

Lindsey Vonn

American Lindsey Vonn is one of the most exciting and **successful** skiers in history. She has more victories than any other female skier.

After winning her eighth World Championships medal, Lindsey retired in 2019.

Family business

Lindsey's father and grandfather were both competitive skiers. She followed in their ski tracks and took to the slopes when she was just **two** years old! By nine she was competing internationally.

Iron will

Lindsey's success has never come easily. She had to overcome several serious **injuries** that almost ended her career, but she worked hard and came back to win.

I famously tell people that I hate the cold!

Career highlights

Skiing World Cup trophy

4 Lindsey is one of only two women to win four World Cup titles.

She was the first American woman to win downhill gold at the Olympics. **1**

Lindsey won a stunning 82 victories during her career—the second most of all time.

Slalom

6 She is one of only six women to have won World Cup races in all five types of ski race.

She competed at the Skiing World Cup at the age of 16. **16**

Yuna Kim

The South Korean superstar Yuna Kim is one of the best and most **loved** athletes in the world.

Yuna uses her fame and success to help others and has donated lots of money to charity.

Pure talent

When Yuna started skating at the age of six, she had to train in old rinks and wore ill-fitting skates. But her talent shone through and she became Korea's national champion at 12 and **world junior champion** at 18.

Skating superstar

Yuna became the first woman to win **all four** of ice-skating's grand slam titles: the Winter Olympics, the World Championships, the Four Continents Championships, and the Grand Prix final.

When she was 16, Yuna moved to **VANCOUVER, CANADA,** to train on the ice rinks there.

Yuna retired after the 2014 Winter Olympics when she was just 23. Four years later, she was chosen to light the cauldron during the opening ceremony for the Winter Olympics in Korea.

At the 2010 Olympic Games in Vancouver, Yuna won gold and set a **NEW WORLD RECORD.**

Usain Bolt

He's not quite as fast as a bolt of lightning, but Usain Bolt is still the **fastest man** in history and the greatest sprinter of all time.

Born to run

Usain was born in Jamaica in 1986 and was a gifted sprinter from a young age. When he was 15 he won gold in the 200m at the World Junior Championships. He was the youngest world junior gold medalist ever, and he was just **getting started**...

The Lightning Bolt

Usain made history at the 2008 Olympics in Beijing, China, when he broke the 100m and 200m **world records**. He was also in record-breaking form at the 2009 World Championships in Berlin, Germany, breaking both records once again!

As a child, Usain was also a fantastic cricket and soccer player.

Usain took his famous celebration pose from a Jamaican tourism ad. It means "to the world."

Usain donated money to protect animals in Kenya, such as the cheetah—the fastest land animal on Earth.

Usain once set the 100m world record even though one of his shoelaces was untied.

Career highlights

9.58 He holds the 100m world record of 9.58 seconds.

He holds the 200m world record of 19.19 seconds. **19.19**

8 He has 8 Olympic gold medals.

11 He won 11 gold medals at the World Championships.

His career top speed is 27.8mph (44.72kph). **27.8**

He's still not as fast as me!

He's the fastest person in human history!

Won in Athens in 2004

Won in Beijing in 2008

Michael **Phelps**

With **23 gold medals**, American swimmer Michael Phelps is the most successful athlete ever to compete in the Olympics.

During training, Michael swam for around five hours every day.

The rise of Phelps

Michael started swimming at the age of seven and qualified for the 2000 Olympic Games when he was just **15 years old**. His record-breaking streak began four years later.

Going for gold

Michael won **six gold medals** at the 2004 Olympics. Four years later, he set the record for most gold medals won at a single games with **eight**. The gold rush continued with **four** in 2012, and the superstar ended his career in style by winning **five** in 2016.

EAT, SLEEP, and SWIM. That's all I do!

Fuel for the machine

All that swimming takes a lot of energy. Michael's eating habits are the stuff of legend. This is what he ate every day while training for the 2008 Olympics.

A five-egg omelet

Two cups of coffee

Three fried eggs, ham, and cheese sandwiches

A pizza

Two ham and cheese sandwiches

Three chocolate-chip pancakes

A bowl of grits

Slices of French toast

Energy drinks

Two bowls of pasta

189

Muhammad Ali

Known as "**The Greatest**," Muhammad Ali was one of the most famous boxers of all time and one of the **best-known figures** of the 20th century.

Ali used to predict which round he would win his fights in, and he was often right!

Cassius Clay

Muhammad was born **Cassius Clay** and took up boxing at age 12. He became famous when he won a **gold medal** at the 1960 Olympics.

Name change

After returning from the Olympics, he changed his name to **Muhammad Ali**. He became world heavyweight champion for the first time in **1964**, winning the Championship belt.

World Championship belt

Around 1 BILLION people watched his famous "Rumble in the Jungle" fight.

Ali's boxing style was all about speed. He famously said he "floats like a butterfly and stings like a bee."

Boxing legend

He was stripped of his titles in 1967 after **refusing to fight** in the Vietnam War because of his religion. But he returned to boxing in 1970 and went on to win **two** more titles.

Muhammad Ali is a hero to many, not just for his boxing skills, but for also standing up for what he believed in.

Lin Dan

China's Lin Dan started playing badminton when he was just five years old. He grew up to become the greatest player of **all time** and a sporting icon.

Lin Dan has won the

Lin was born in Longyan, China, in 1983.

The greatest

Lin became a professional badminton player as a teenager. By the time he was 19, he was **world number one**. He holds many records, including being the only men's player to win back-to-back Olympic titles.

All England Open

World Cup

Thomas Cup

Asian Championships

Asian Games

Sudirman Cup

Super Series Masters Finals

Lin's parents wanted him to play the piano when he was young, but he gave that up to focus on badminton.

World Championships FIVE TIMES!

Super Dan's Super Slam

Famously nicknamed "**Super Dan**" by one of his rivals, Lin is the only player in history to win **all nine** of badminton's major titles (known as the Super Slam).

193

Lionel Messi

Lionel Messi is thought of by many as the finest soccer player of his generation and, by some, as the **best of all time**.

Early life

Lionel was born in **Argentina** in 1987. As a child he suffered from a medical problem that slowed his growth. However, it was clear Lionel was super talented, and at 12, he was given a tryout by the Spanish club Barcelona.

Barcelona was so impressed by Lionel's skill that the club offered to pay for his medicine.

Messi's nickname is "The Flea" because his quick, darting style makes him a pest to defenders!

Lionel Messi has played more than 600 games

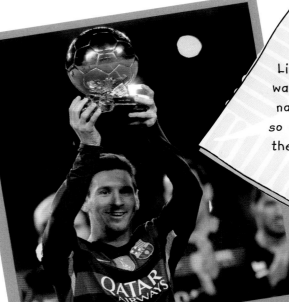

Messi has won the Ballon d'Or, the award given to the world's best player, five times.

Lionel's first contract was written on a paper napkin! Barcelona was so amazed at his talent, the club wanted to sign him right away.

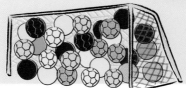

91 In 2012, he scored 91 goals for Barcelona and Argentina.

9 He has won the award for the best player in the Spanish league a record nine times.

400 He is the only player to score more than 400 goals in the Spanish league.

68 He is Argentina's all-time top goal scorer, with 68.

Lionel moved to Spain and signed with Barcelona. The rest is history!

21 In 2012 and 2013, he scored in 21 Spanish league matches in a row.

Career of a champion

Lionel made his debut for Barcelona at age 17 and has gone on to win a staggering number of titles with the club, including the Spanish league title 10 times and the Champions League four times.

10 Like many soccer legends, he wears the number 10.

in his career with Barcelona.

Donald
Bradman

Australian Donald Bradman is a cricketing **legend**. One of his records is so impressive, it's called one of the greatest achievements in any sport.

Batting average

99.94

Batting average

In cricket and baseball, batting average measures how **successful** a batsman, or batter, is. In cricket, it's the number of runs scored divided by the number of times the batsman is gotten out.

The next best average after Donald's 99.94 is 61.87, by Australia's Adam Voges.

The Don

Donald first played for Australia in 1928, age 20, and became the best batsman in the game. He was almost unstoppable during his 20 year career.

Australia

Donald became a national icon in Australia. He even had a stamp and coin made in his honor.

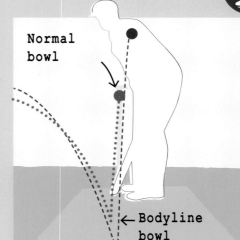

Normal bowl

← Bodyline bowl

Beating bodyline

To try to beat Donald, Australia's rival, England, resorted to a tactic called "bodyline" (aiming at the batsman instead of the wicket). They won that game, but Donald had the last laugh. He never lost to England again.

Sir Donald Bradman
20 cents

↖ Adam Voges

When he was young, Donald practiced with a cricket stump for a bat and a golf ball.

LeBron James

Known as "**King James**," LeBron

James is considered to be one of the best **basketball** players of all time.

LeBron was born in Akron, Ohio. It was clear from a young age that he was very talented. By 16, he was on the cover of magazines around the country.

The rise of the King

When he was 18, LeBron became the **youngest player** to be chosen first in the NBA (National Basketball Association) draft. Best of all, he was picked by his local team, the **Cleveland Cavaliers**, and quickly became one of the game's best players.

Team change

After several years playing in Cleveland, he moved to the **Miami Heat** and won two NBA Championships in 2012 and 2013. He rejoined the **Cavaliers** in 2014 and led the team to its first Championship in 2016, before joining the **LA Lakers** in 2018.

LeBron is also famous for helping others. He has set up a school called "I Promise" in his hometown of Akron, Ohio, to help children in need.

Career highlights

1 Youngest player to be the number 1 pick in the NBA draft.

2 Two Olympic gold medals with USA's basketball team.

3 Three-time NBA Champion.

4 Currently fourth on the NBA's all-time points-scoring list.

4 Voted the NBA's Most Valuable Player four times.

Sporting **events**

What do you get when you bring the best teams and players **together**? Lots and lots of exciting competitions! All over the world, people come together to take part in or watch athletes compete in special events. One reason is to see who is the best, but mostly, it's a lot of fun!

The Olympics

The Summer Olympic Games are the world's most famous **sporting event**. The top athletes from around the world come together to see who is the best of the **best**.

More than just sports

Although the sports are the main reason to come together, the Olympics are special for more than just the competition. It's a time when the whole world **celebrates** together.

Old and new

The Olympics were inspired by ancient Olympic Games held in Greece many years ago. Frenchman **Pierre de Coubertin** was the driving force behind bringing the Olympics back.

The modern Games were held for the first time in Athens, Greece, in 1896.

Pierre de Coubertin

The Olympics in figures:

Held every

4

years

33

different sports

339

events

1

huge celebration!

The 2020 Games in Tokyo were the first

1988
Seoul,
Korea

1992
Barcelona,
Spain

1996
Atlanta,
USA

2000
Sydney,
Australia

2004
Athens,
Greece

2008
Beijing,
China

2012
London,
UK

2016
Rio de
Janeiro,
Brazil

2020
Tokyo,
Japan

Hosting

The Olympics are held every four years and are staged in a different **city** each time to symbolize countries working together and to celebrate different cultures.

Olympic flame

A **torch** carrying fire from the site of the ancient games in Olympia, Greece, is passed from person to person, all the way to where the games are held. The torch is used to light a big fire that burns during the Olympic Games.

At the first modern Olympics, winners were awarded an olive branch. But since 1904, they are given gold, silver, and bronze medals for coming first, second, and third.

American swimmer Michael Phelps is the most successful Olympic athlete in history. He won an amazing 23 gold medals during his career.

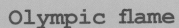

games to have **SKATEBOARDING** as an Olympic sport.

The Winter Olympics

Just like the Summer Games, the Winter Olympic Games are held every **four years**. But all the sports take place on **snow** and **ice**.

The Winter Games have been held in 12 different countries across Europe, North America, and Asia.

History of the Games

The Games were held for the first time in 1924, in **Chamonix**, France. Until 1992, the Summer and Winter Games were held in the **same year**, but now run two years apart.

Ice hockey

Past

The 2018 Winter Olympic Games were held in **Pyeongchang, South Korea**, and included:

from
92
countries

across
7
sports

2,833
competitors

competing in
102
events

50
of which involved skiing

1994
Lillehammer,
Norway

1998
Nagano,
Japan

2002
Salt Lake
City, USA

2006
Turin,
Italy

2010
Vancouver,
Canada

2014
Sochi,
Russia

2018
Pyeongchang,
South Korea

2022
Beijing,
China

Bobsled

Norwegian dominance

No country has performed as well at the Winter Olympics as **Norway**. Norwegian athletes lead the all-time medal table, in both gold medals (132) and overall medals (368).

Norwegian cross-country skier Marit Bjørgen is the most successful Winter Olympian ever. She has won 15 medals (8 golds).

Marit
Bjørgen

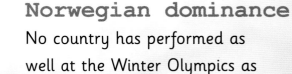

Future

The 2022 games will be held in **Beijing, China**; 109 events will take place across seven sports:

Biathlon
Bobsled
Curling
Ice hockey

Luge
Skating
Skiing

The Paralympic Games

The Paralympic Games are an **international sports competition** for disabled athletes held every four years. There are both Summer and Winter Paralympics.

Origins

In 1948, Sir Ludwig Guttmann organized a sports competition at a hospital in England for soldiers who had suffered injuries while fighting during **World War II**. Four years later, competitors from the Netherlands joined the Games and the Paralympic movement was born.

Most of the sports played at the Paralympics are the same as the ones at the Olympics. But a few, such as "goalball" and "boccia," are unique to the Paralympics.

American Trischa Zorn is the most successful Paralympian in history. She won an amazing 41 gold medals in swimming between 1980 and 2004.

The Games

The first Games for disabled athletes were held in Rome, Italy, in 1960. Today, the Paralympics are staged **at the same place** as the Summer and Winter Olympic Games. They are an important part of the world's sporting calendar.

The "Para" in "Paralympics" comes from the Greek word "para," which means "next to," because the Paralympics run alongside the Olympics.

Prosthetic leg

The events

The Paralympics feature more than 20 sports and hundreds of events, including track and field, wheelchair basketball, cycling, swimming, and wheelchair fencing. The athletes range from those who are blind, to those who have lost a limb or use a wheelchair, and many more.

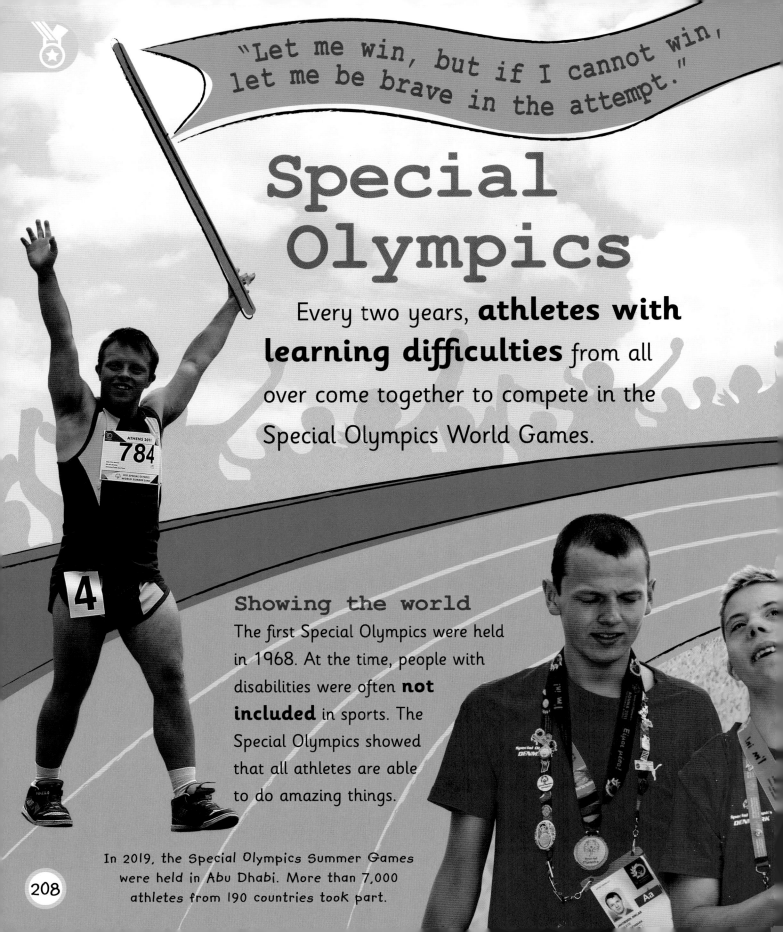

"Let me win, but if I cannot win, let me be brave in the attempt."

Special Olympics

Every two years, **athletes with learning difficulties** from all over come together to compete in the Special Olympics World Games.

Showing the world

The first Special Olympics were held in 1968. At the time, people with disabilities were often **not included** in sports. The Special Olympics showed that all athletes are able to do amazing things.

In 2019, the Special Olympics Summer Games were held in Abu Dhabi. More than 7,000 athletes from 190 countries took part.

Eunice Kennedy Shriver

The Games are held every two years, but the Special Olympics community helps children and adults with learning difficulties get into sports all year round.

Camp Shriver

The Games were the idea of American **Eunice Kennedy Shriver**. In the 1960s, Eunice found out that children with learning difficulties often weren't accepted into summer camps. So she held her own special **summer camp** at her farm.

There are around 200 million people with learning difficulties all around the world.

There are winter and summer Special Olympic World Games.

209

The World Cup

The World Cup is a huge **international soccer** tournament held every **four years** to decide which country's team is the best.

The world's biggest stage

There's nothing that captures people's attention more than the World Cup. Around **3.5 billion** people watched the 2018 World Cup. That's around **half of all the people in the world!**

Stages

The World Cup was first held in **1930** in Uruguay. The competition is made up of two parts: a **group stage** and a **knockout phase**. Today, 32 teams play for a chance to win, but as of 2026, 48 teams will enter.

The World Cup trophy

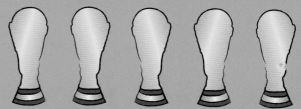

Brazil has won the World Cup a record five times.

Only eight countries have won the men's World Cup:

Brazil (five times)
Italy (four times)
Germany (four times)
France (twice)
Uruguay (twice)
Argentina (twice)
England (once)
Spain (once)

Only four countries have won the Women's World Cup:

USA (four times)
Germany (twice)
Japan (once)
Norway (once)

Women's World Cup

The FIFA Women's World Cup was first held in **1991**.
Like the men's competition, it is staged every four years.
The **United States** has been the most successful team, winning **four times**.

The Super Bowl

The Super Bowl is the game that decides who will be **football's** champion. Thirty-two teams vie for the title, but only one can win.

All or nothing

The Super Bowl takes place on the first Sunday in February. It is played after a 16-game season that is followed by **playoff** games, where teams are eliminated when they lose. The last two remaining teams face off in the Super Bowl.

The 2015 Super Bowl between the New England Patriots and the Seattle Seahawks was watched by 114.4 million people!

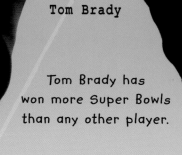

Tom Brady

Tom Brady has won more Super Bowls than any other player.

The prize

The trophy given to the Super Bowl winner is the "Vince Lombardi Trophy." It's named after the legendary **coach** who won the first two Super Bowls.

Vince Lombardi Trophy

During halftime, musicians perform a spectacular concert. Advertisers pay millions for commerical spots during breaks.

More food is eaten on the US on Super Bowl Sunday than on any other day except Thanksgiving.

Green Bay Packers

Sunday showdown

The first Super Bowl was played in 1961 between the **Green Bay Packers** and the **Kansas City Chiefs**. The day of the Super Bowl has become known as "**Super Bowl Sunday**."

Kansas City Chiefs

Indianapolis 500

The Indianapolis 500, also known as the **Indy 500**, is the world's **oldest motor race**. It was first held in 1911.

History of the Indy

The race is held every May at the Indianapolis Motor Speedway in Indiana. The race is long and tiring and takes around **three hours** to finish. Drivers need to be skilled and have great concentration.

Vroom! Vroom!

Why 500?
The oval-shaped circuit is **2.5 miles (4km)** long. Drivers race **200 laps**, which is a distance of **500 miles (800km)**. That's why it's called the Indy 500!

The race was shown on TELEVISION for the first time in 1965. Before that, it could only be followed on the RADIO.

Every year since the 1930s, the winner of the race celebrates by drinking a bottle of milk or pouring it over their head!

The Indy 500, the Monaco Grand Prix, and 24 Hours of Le Mans make up "The Triple Crown of Motorsport."

Most wins

Three American drivers are tied for the record of most wins, with **four.**

A.J. Foyt

Al Unser

Rick Mears

Tour de France

The Tour de France is the most famous cycling event in the world. It's **very difficult** and **tiring**, with some parts taking place on mountains.

The race is made up of different **stages**. Overall, it takes three weeks and goes for thousands of miles. The route is different every year, but it always finishes in Paris.

While most of the race takes place in France, sometimes

Eddy Merckx from Belgium, Bernard Hinault and Jacques Anquetil from France, and Miguel Induráin from Spain, have all won the Tour de France **five times**.

Eddy Merckx is a cycling legend. He holds the record for **most stage wins** in the Tour de France, with 34.

Eddy Merckx →

216

Jerseys

Riders who are leading certain categories wear special **colored jerseys** during the race:

The race's leading sprinter wears green.

The overall leader wears yellow.

The leading rider in the mountain stages wears polka dots.

The first Tour de France was in 1903. Cyclists stopped at cafés to rest.

the stages pass through other countries.

In 1989, after 2,041 miles (3,285km), the winner, Greg LeMond, finished just **8 seconds** ahead of the cyclist behind him. It was the **closest race** in Tour de France history.

Frenchman Sylvain Chavanel holds the record for Tour de France **appearances**, with 18.

← Sylvain Chavanel

The Grand Slams

The tennis season is built around **four** major tournaments, known as "Grand Slams." To win each Slam, players must win seven straight matches against the best players in the world.

The Australian Open

Played in Melbourne in January, the Australian Open used to be played on grass, but is now played on a **hard court**.

Germany's Steffi Graf set a record by reaching 13 Grand Slam finals in a row.

Steffi Graf →

The French Open

The **red clay** surface of the French Open slows the ball and makes it **bounce higher**. This is good for players who strike the ball with lots of power. It's played in Paris in June.

Rafael Nadal

Spain's Rafael Nadal is the king of clay. He has won the French Open an extraordinary 12 times!

Around 50,000 balls are used at each of the Grand Slams!

The most successful men's and women's singles players are Switzerland's Roger Federer, with 20 titles, and Australia's Margaret Court, with 24.

Wimbledon

The oldest and most famous Grand Slam is Wimbledon, played in July in England. It's the only Slam played on **grass**, which is the **fastest** and least bouncy tennis surface.

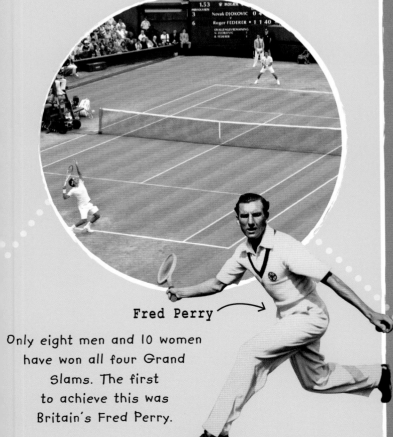

Fred Perry

Only eight men and 10 women have won all four Grand Slams. The first to achieve this was Britain's Fred Perry.

The US Open

Naomi Osaka

Like the Australian Open, the US Open is played on a **hard court**, which is faster than clay but slower than grass. It's played in New York in September.

Index

Acknowledgments

The publisher would like to thank the following for their kind permission to reproduce their photographs:

Key: a= above; b=below/bottom; c=center; f=far; l=left, r=right, t=top.

1 Alamy Stock Photo: Yolanda Oltra (cra). **Dreamstime. com:** Neil Lockhart (cb); Raja Rc / Rcmathiraj (b). **Getty Images:** Chris Elise / NBAE (l). **2 Alamy Stock Photo:** TGSPHOTO (bl). **Dreamstime.com:** Volodymyr Melnyk (br); Stephen Noakes (bc). **Getty Images:** Stanislav Krasilnikov\TASS (cr). **2-3 Dreamstime.com:** Raja Rc / Rcmathiraj (b). **3 123RF.com:** Roman Stetsyk (cb). **Alamy Stock Photo:** Artokoloro Quint Lox Limited (cl). **Dreamstime.com:** Skypixel (cr). **iStockphoto.com:** pidjoe (bl). **4 Dreamstime. com:** Sergeyoch (tr); Roman Stetsyk (cb). **Getty Images:** Baptiste Fernandez / Icon Sport (br). **5 Dreamstime.com:** Artisticco Llc (tr). **Getty Images:** TF-Images (bc). **6 123RF. com:** Fabio Pagani (cb). **Alamy Stock Photo:** Cultura Creative (RF) (br); sportpoint (clb). **Dreamstime.com:** Walter Arce (bc). **Getty Images:** Wally McNamee / Corbis (cra). **7 Getty Images:** Ben Stansall / AFP (tl); Denis Doyle / TPN (bc). **8 Dreamstime.com:** Branchecarica (cla); Vladimir Kulakov (c). **Getty Images:** Foto Olimpik / NurPhoto (cla/Speedway). **8-9 123RF.com:** Marina Scurupii (Background). **9 Dreamstime.com:** Petesaloutos (ca); Skypixel (bc). **Getty Images:** Jamie McDonald (cl). **12-13 Dreamstime.com:** Montypeter (Background). **13 Alamy Stock Photo:** Entertainment Pictures (crb). **14-15 Alamy Stock Photo:** Cultura Creative (RF) (c). **15 Dreamstime.com:** Volodymyr Melnyk (cl). **16 Getty Images:** Mark Brake (c). **16-17 Alamy Stock Photo:** wanderworldimages (Background). **17 Getty Images:** Michael Dodge (cla). **18-19 Getty Images:** Mike Hewitt. **19 Getty Images:** Adrian Dennis / AFP (br). **20 iStockphoto.com:** benoitb (crb). **20-21 Dreamstime. com:** Raja Rc / Rcmathiraj (cb). **21 iStockphoto.com:** pidjoe (c); strickke (cra). **22-23 Alamy Stock Photo:** Hero Images Inc. (cb). **Dreamstime.com:** Montypeter (Background). **23 Alamy Stock Photo:** Hero Images Inc. (cla). **24 Alamy Stock Photo:** TGSPHOTO (cra). **Dreamstime.com:** Wavebreakmedia Ltd (bl). **Getty Images:** Alex Davidson (l). **24-25 Dreamstime.com:** Ritu Jethani (t/Background); Raja Rc / Rcmathiraj (b/Background). 25 **123RF.com:** Ilyas Dean (br). **Alamy Stock Photo:** Mitchell Gunn / ESPA (cl). **Dreamstime.com:** Stephen Noakes (clb). **Getty Images:** Alex Davidson (crb); Michael Steele (cr). **26 Getty Images:** Juice Images (ca). **26-27 123RF.com:** Sirapob Konjay (t). **Dreamstime.com:** Rangizzz (c/Background). **27 Alamy Stock Photo:** Historic Collection (cl). **29 Dreamstime.com:** Jerry Coli (tr); Skypixel (bc, crb). **30 Getty Images:** Steve Christo / Corbis (cla). **30-31 123RF.com:** Vereshchagin Dmitry (Background). **Alamy Stock Photo:** Ilyas Ayub. **31 Dreamstime.com:** Andreykuzmin (r). **32 Dreamstime. com:** Eugene Onischenko (r). **33 123RF.com:** Volodymyr Melnyk (cr). **Alamy Stock Photo:** Martin Berry (cr). **Rex by Shutterstock:** Kiyoshi Ota / EPA-EFE (cla). **34-35 Dreamstime.com:** Pixattitude (c). **35 Alamy Stock Photo:** Simon Balson (ca). **39 Alamy Stock Photo:** Age Fotostock (clb); Dipper Historic (crb). **Dorling Kindersley:** American Museum of Natural History (bc). **Dreamstime.com:** Vladimir Galkin (cl). **40-41 Dreamstime.com:** Montypeter (t). **Getty Images:** Dimitri Iundt / Corbis / VCG (bc). **40 Getty Images:** Tony Duffy / Allsport (bc); Dimitri Iundt / Corbis / VCG (c); Alexander Hassenstein (bl); Quinn Rooney (br). **41 Getty Images:** Kamil Krzaczynski / AFP (br/New); Remy Gros / Icon Sport (bl); Dursun Aydemir / Anadolu Agency (bc). **42-43 Dreamstime.com:** Petesaloutos (c). **iStockphoto. com:** Kerrick (t/Background). **43 Alamy Stock Photo:** Federico Caputo (bl). **Getty Images:** Robert Riger (ca). **44 Dreamstime.com:** Yoshiro Mizuta (cl). **Getty Images:** Manuel Blondeau / Icon Sport (cla). **45 Alamy Stock Photo:** UpperCut Images (ca). **Getty Images:** Dimitri Iundt / Corbis / VCG (crb). **46 Dreamstime.com:** Dariusz

Kopestynski / Copestello (bc); Hkratky (cl); Mitchell Gunn (cr). **47 Alamy Stock Photo:** Action Plus Sports (tr). **Dreamstime.com:** Evren Kalinbacak (cl). **48 Alamy Stock Photo:** Wang Lili / Xinhua (r). **49 Alamy Stock Photo:** INTERFOTO (l); Jordi Salas (tr). **50-51 123RF.com:** Vassiliy Prikhodko (t). **Getty Images:** Cameron Spencer (c). **51 Alamy Stock Photo:** Richard Grange (cl). **Getty Images:** Lennart Preiss (crb). **52 Dreamstime.com:** Chelsdo (cra); Ukrphoto (cl); Roman Stetsyk (c); Petrjoura (b). **53 123RF. com:** Roman Stetsyk (tl). **Dreamstime.com:** Igor Dolgov (clb); Ukrphoto (crb). **Getty Images:** Matthias Hangst / Bongarts (cb); Visual China Group (tr). **54 123RF.com:** ostill (fcra). **Getty Images:** Jamie Cross / Jamie_cross (cb); Pixattitude (cra). **55 Alamy Stock Photo:** Cyclist People By Vision (ca). **Dreamstime.com:** Pixattitude (cra, tr); Rudy Umans / Rudyumans (bc). **56 Getty Images:** Dan Mullan (clb). **56-57 iStockphoto.com:** Henrik5000. **57 Getty Images:** Martin Barraud (cr); Alexander Hassenstein / Bongarts (cl). **58 123RF.com:** Abdul Razak Latif (cl); Fabio Pagani (cb). **Dreamstime.com:** Branchecarica (tr); Neil Lockhart (ca); Anan Punyod (cb/Road). **Getty Images:** MediaNews Group (bl); Ian Walton (crb). **58-59 Getty Images:** Foto Olimpik / NurPhoto (t). **59 123RF.com:** mreco99 (cr). **Dreamstime.com:** Walter Arce (br); Ievgen Soloviov (cb); Pavel Boruta (cl); Anan Punyod (br/Road). **60 Getty Images:** Andy Lyons (cra). **60-61 Getty Images:** Natasha Morello / Racing Photos. **62-63 123RF.com:** Sirapob Konjay (t). **Dreamstime.com:** Andreevaee (cb). **62 123RF.com:** martinkay78 (cb); Natthawut panyosaeng (cl). **63 123RF.com:** Natthawut panyosaeng (cl). **Dorling Kindersley:** Barnabas Kindersley (cla). **Getty Images:** TF-Images (cr). **64 Alamy Stock Photo:** PhotoStock-Israel (cl). **Dreamstime.com:** Eugene Onischenko (crb); Piyathep (tr). **Getty Images:** Nao Imai / Aflo (c). **65 123RF.com:** olegdudko (b). **Alamy Stock Photo:** Ivan Okyere-Boakye Photography (tl). **Dreamstime.com:** Volodymyr Melnyk (cl). **Getty Images:** The Asahi Shimbun (tr). **iStockphoto.com:** Mrbig_Photography (bc). **66 123RF.com:** Andrii Kaderov (clb). **66-67 123RF.com:** ocusfocus (c). **67 123RF.com:** Vasilis Ververidis (c). **Dreamstime.com:** Lumppini (tc). **68-69 Alamy Stock Photo:** Peter Llewellyn. **70 Getty Images:** Hoang Dinh Nam / AFP (tl). **71 Dreamstime.com:** Kanjanee Chaisin (cla). **Getty Images:** Visual China Group. **72 123RF.com:** Attila Mittl / atee83 (tl). **72-73 Getty Images:** Baptiste Fernandez / Icon Sport. **74 Dreamstime.com:** Galina Barskaya (crb); .shock (cl). **74-75 Dreamstime.com:** Sergeyoch (b). **75 Alamy Stock Photo:** Cal Sport Media (l). **76 123RF.com:** Anan Kaewkhammul (c). **77 Dorling Kindersley:** South of England Rare Breeds Centre, Ashford, Kent (cla). **Dreamstime.com:** Pariyawit Sukumpantanasarn (cra); Zagorskid (tl, bc). **79 Alamy Stock Photo:** Cultura Creative (RF). **Getty Images:** Mike Brett / Popperfoto (cra). **80 Dorling Kindersley:** Stephen Oliver (tr). **Rex by Shutterstock:** Andy Wong / AP (clb). **80-81 Dreamstime. com:** Eugene Onischenko (r). **81 Dorling Kindersley:** Stephen Oliver (cr). **82-83 Alamy Stock Photo:** Hemis. **83 Rex by Shutterstock:** Andrew Cowie (cr). **84 Getty Images:** Jordan Mansfield (crb). **86 123RF.com:** ammit (bc). **87 123RF.com:** Alexutemov (tc). **Dreamstime.com:** Levente Gyori (bl). **88-89 Alamy Stock Photo:** Yolanda Oltra (t). **Dreamstime.com:** Jin Peng (Background). **88 Alamy Stock Photo:** Hilary Morgan (crb). **89 Alamy Stock Photo:** TCD / Prod.DB (cb). **90 Dreamstime.com:** Trekandshoot (crb). **Getty Images:** Jamie McDonald (r). **91 123RF.com:** lzflzf (ca). **Alamy Stock Photo:** Brian Lowe / ZUMA Wire (cb). **92-93 iStockphoto.com:** Lorado (t). **93 Alamy Stock Photo:** Dinodia Photos (cra); Janine Wiedel Photolibrary (cla). **94 123RF.com:** Allan Swart (cl, cr). **94-95 Dreamstime.com:** Adam88x (cb/Background); Albund (t/Background). **95 123RF.com:** Allan Swart (c). **Dreamstime.com:** Oocoskun (crb, bc). **96 Getty Images:** moodboard (ca). **97 Dreamstime.com:** Astrofireball (cra).

Getty Images: Thomas Northcut / Photodisc (cla). **98 Dreamstime.com:** Parkinsonsniper (br). **Getty Images:** The Asahi Shimbun (bc). **99 Alamy Stock Photo:** Stephen Barnes (bl); Sueddeutsche Zeitung Photo (cr); Barry Lewis (br). **102 Dreamstime.com:** Beat Glauser / Hoschi (Background). **103 Alamy Stock Photo:** Hiroyuki Sato / AFLO (cb). **Dreamstime.com:** Danyliuk (tr); Miramisska (tl). **104 Dreamstime.com:** Gibsonff (cb); Miramisska (cb/Snowman). **104-105 123RF.com:** Pakhnyushchyy (Background). **105 Getty Images:** Kim Stallknecht (cl). **106 Getty Images:** Alexander Hassenstein / Bongarts. **107 Dreamstime.com:** Artisticco Llc (cl). **Getty Images:** Jonathan Nackstrand / AFP (br); Adam Pretty / Bongarts (tr). **108 Getty Images:** Daniel Milchev (c). **108-109 Getty Images:** Laurent Salino / Agence Zoom (cb). **iStockphoto.com:** Evilknevil. **109 Dreamstime.com:** Andreykuzmin (tr). **Getty Images:** Tom Pennington (crb). **110 Getty Images:** Dean Mouhtaropoulos - International Skating Union (ISU) / ISU (clb); Christof Koepsel - International Skating Union (ISU) / ISU (cb). **111 Alamy Stock Photo:** Newscom (cra). **Dreamstime.com:** Vladimir Kulakov. **Getty Images:** Tim De Waele (crb). **112-113 123RF.com:** Marina Scurupii (cb). **112 123RF.com:** Dmitry Kalinovsky (cr). **Alamy Stock Photo:** Nordicphotos (cl). **113 Alamy Stock Photo:** Everett Collection Inc (cra); Peter Horree (tl). **Getty Images:** Stanislav Krasilnikov\TASS (tc). **114-115 123RF.com:** Jon Schulte (c/Background). **Alamy Stock Photo:** ITAR-TASS News Agency. **Dreamstime.com:** Martinmark (cb/Background). **Getty Images:** Gabriel Bouys / AFP (t/Background). **114 Alamy Stock Photo:** Lorraine Swanson (clb). **115 Alamy Stock Photo:** Michael Bush (cr). **116 iStockphoto.com:** Dmytro Aksonov. **117 Alamy Stock Photo:** imageBROKER (ca, cra); Alexander Piragis (cr). **118-119 Dreamstime.com:** Martinmark (cb). **Getty Images:** Henning Bagger / AFP (c). **119 Getty Images:** Gary M Prior / Allsport (tr). **122 123RF.com:** Aleksey Satyrenko (cr). **Getty Images:** Alessandro Garofalo / Action Plus (cl). **122-123 Getty Images:** The Asahi Shimbun. **123 123RF.com:** Benoit Daoust (tr); Aleksandr Markin (cr). **Alamy Stock Photo:** Westend61 GmbH (cl). **Getty Images:** Huw Fairclough (tc). **124-125 Dreamstime.com:** Tanwalai Silp Aran (t); Issaranupong Chaimongkol / Imooba (b/Background). **Getty Images:** Ferenc Isza / AFP (ca); David Eulitt / Kansas City Star / Tribune News Service (cb). **126 123RF.com:** Vladimir Ovchinnikov (l). **Dreamstime.com:** Tropicdreams (cr). **127 Alamy Stock Photo:** Calamy Stock Images (cr). **Dreamstime.com:** Epicstock. **128 Alamy Stock Photo:** Artokoloro Quint Lox Limited (cl). **Getty Images:** James Worsfold (clb). **128-129 Getty Images:** James Worsfold. **129 Alamy Stock Photo:** Cavan (crb). **130-131 Getty Images:** Leo Mason - Split Second / Corbis. **131 Getty Images:** Ullstein Bild (tr). **132-133 Alamy Stock Photo:** Hero Images Inc. **133 Alamy Stock Photo:** Allstar Picture Library (cra). **134-135 Depositphotos Inc:** geoffchilds. **135 Alamy Stock Photo:** Tasfoto (tr). **Getty Images:** Jean-Michel Andre / AFP (cr). **136 123RF.com:** Epicstockmedia (br). **137 Dreamstime.com:** Mike K. / Mikekwok (br). **140 Alamy Stock Photo:** Cavan Images (cr). **Bridgeman Images:** Egyptian / Fitzwilliam Museum, University of Cambridge, UK (bl). **141 Alamy Stock Photo:** Age Fotostock (cb); Historic Collection (cr); World History Archive (br). **Bridgeman Images:** Aztec, (16th century) / Private Collection (cla). **142 123RF.com:** smokhov (c/Background). **Dreamstime.com:** Sabelskaya (cb). **143 123RF.com:** smokhov (bl). **Dreamstime.com:** Wavebreakmedia Ltd (bc). **144 123RF.com:** PaylessImages (bc). **145 Dorling Kindersley:** Natural History Museum, London (tr, cr); Stephen Oliver (clb). **146 Alamy Stock Photo:** kpzfoto (cb). **146-147 Alamy Stock Photo:** Findlay. **148-149 Getty Images:** Matthias Hangst / Bongarts. **150 Dreamstime.com:** Dodgeball (crb). **151 Alamy Stock Photo:** MBI (l, cr). **Dreamstime.com:** Dodgeball (tr); Monkey Business Images (c). **152 Fotolia:** DenisNata (ca). **153 Alamy Stock Photo:** Granger Historical Picture Archive (cra). **154 123RF.com:** Rattasaritt phloysungwarn (cl, bc). **155 Dreamstime.com:** Andersastphoto (br); Axel Bueckert (cra). **156 Alamy Stock Photo:** Granger Historical Picture Archive (cla); KEYSTONE Pictures USA (c). **Getty Images:** Wally McNamee / Corbis (bl). **157 Dreamstime.com:** Paul Topp / Nalukai (cra). **158 Getty Images:** Popperfoto (bl). **159 Dreamstime.com:** Sergey Rusakov / F4f (cra). **Getty Images:** Keystone-France / Gamma-Keystone (cla); Stephen Pond (crb); Simone Kuhlmey / Pacific Press / LightRocket (cb). **160 Dreamstime.com:** Dmitry Pichugin / Dmitryp (clb). **161 Alamy Stock Photo:** Granger Historical Picture Archive (t); Newscom (clb). **162-163 Alamy Stock Photo:** Nosyrevy (b). **162 Alamy Stock Photo:** Wally McNamee / Corbis (br). Rex by Shutterstock: Paul Vathis / AP (cr). **163 PunchStock:** Westend61 / Rainer Dittrich (tr). **164 Getty Images:** Norman Potter / Central Press (cr). **165 Alamy Stock Photo:** KEYSTONE Pictures USA (l). **166-167 Alamy Stock Photo:** Everett Collection Inc (c). **167 Alamy Stock Photo:** INTERFOTO (crb); Pictorial Press Ltd (cl); United Archives GmbH (cr). **iStockphoto.com:** Nosyrevy (b). **168 Getty Images:** DEA / Biblioteca Ambrosiana (crb). **169 Alamy Stock Photo:** Keystone Pictures USA (l); Science History Images (tr). **Getty Images:** Scott Peterson / Liaison (crb); National Motor Museum / Heritage Images (clb). **170 Dreamstime.com:** RightFramePhotoVideo (tl). **170-171 Dreamstime.com:** Paul Topp / Nalukai. **iStockphoto.com:** Kerrick (t/Background). **171 iStockphoto.com:** YinYang (cr). **172-173 Dreamstime.com:** Reinhold Leitner / Leitnerr (Background). **172 Alamy Stock Photo:** Science History Images (bc). **173 Getty Images:** Hilaria McCarthy / Daily Express / Hulton Archive (br); Photo12 / Universal Images Group (c); General Photographic Agency (tr); Sandra Mu (bc). **174 Getty Images:** Ben Stansall / AFP (ca); Allsport Hulton / Archive (cla); Denis Doyle (cl); Stanley Weston (bc); TPN (br). **175 123RF.com:** Olga Besnard (c). **Getty Images:** Monner (ca); Sergeyoch (bl). **176-177 Getty Images:** TPN. **177 123RF.com:** Oksana Desiatkina (crb). **Dreamstime.com:** Sergeyoch (cb). **Getty Images:** Adam Pretty (l). **178 Alamy Stock Photo:** AF archive (r). **179 Dreamstime.com:** Alhovik (tr); Pincarel (tc); Julián Rovagnati / Erdosain (cra); Excentro (c). **180 Getty Images:** Elsa (cl). **181 Dreamstime.com:** Monner. **182 Alamy Stock Photo:** Action Plus Sports (cl). **182-183 Alamy Stock Photo:** Mauro Dalla Pozza. **183 Alamy Stock Photo:** Pacific Press Agency (r). **184 Dreamstime.com:** Olga Besnard. **185 123RF.com:** Olga Besnard (c). **Dreamstime.com:** Igor Dolgov (clb). **186-187 Getty Images:** Ben Stansall / AFP. **187 123RF.com:** Adamgolabek (tl). **Getty Images:** Simon Maina / AFP (ca); Steve Turner (crb). **188 Getty Images:** Al Bello (clb). **188-189 Getty Images:** Tom Pennington. **189 Getty Images:** Alex Menendez (bl). **190 Getty Images:** Jerry Cooke / Sports Illustrated (cl); Chris Ratcliffe (crb). **191 Getty Images:** Stanley Weston (l). **192-193 Alamy Stock Photo:** Xu Chang / Xinhua. **193 Dreamstime.com:** Pariyawit Sukumpantanasarn (r). **194 Getty Images:** Denis Doyle (r). **194-195 Dreamstime.com:** Raja Rc / Rcmathiraj. **195 Alamy Stock Photo:** Pau Barrena / Xinhua (cla). **196 Getty Images:** Allsport Hulton / Archive (r). **196-197 iStockphoto.com:** Kerrick (t/Background). **197 Dreamstime.com:** Stephen Noakes (tr). **Getty Images:** Paul Kane (l). **198-199 Getty Images:** Chris Elise / NBAE (b). **198 Alamy Stock Photo:** Michael Mcelroy / ZUMA Wire (tl). **199 Alamy Stock Photo:** Storms Media Group (tc). **200-201 Getty Images:** Leontura (t). **200 Alamy Stock Photo:** Everett Collection Inc (cra). Pedro Ugarte / AFP (bl). **201 Getty Images:** Chris Graythen (cla); Vladimir Rys (ca). **202 Alamy Stock Photo:** Archive Pics (crb); Jan Miks (tr). **Getty Images:** Shirley Kwok / Pacific Press / LightRocket (cl). **203 Dreamstime.com:** Lars Christensen / C-foto (cla); Idey (cla/Stadium). **204 Getty Images:** Streeter Lecka (bl). **204-205 Dreamstime.com:** Jin Peng (c/Background). **205 Alamy Stock Photo:** Karl-Josef Hildenbrand / dpa (c). **206 Alamy Stock Photo:** George S de Blonsky (bl). **Getty Images:** Peter Stone / Mirrorpix (br). **206-207 Alamy Stock Photo:** sportpoint (c). **207 Getty Images:** Scott Barbour / ALLSPORT (bl). **208 Getty Images:** Vladimir Rys (l). **208-209 123RF.com:** Kwanchai Chai-udom (t). **Alamy Stock Photo:** Santiago Vidal Vallejo (bc). **Dreamstime.com:** Raja Rc / Rcmathiraj (b/Background). **209 Getty Images:** Reg Lancaster / Daily Express (tr); Vladimir Rys (cr); Wolfgang Kaehler / LightRocket (crb). **210 Getty Images:** Pedro Ugarte / AFP (bl). **210-211 Dreamstime.com:** Elena Chepik (Confetti). **Getty Images:** Gabriel Bouys / AFP (t/Background). **211 Getty Images:** Christopher Morris / Corbis (b). **212 123RF.com:** xsight (r). **213 123RF.com:** Baiba Opule (bc). **Alamy Stock Photo:** Jason Pohuski / CSM (br); Dan Anderson / ZUMAPRESS.com (cra). **Dreamstime.com:** Jakub Gojda (crb); Guido Vrola (c). **Getty Images:** Christopher Evans / MediaNews Group / Boston Herald (cl); Burazin / Photographer's Choice RF (tl); Robin Alam / Icon Sportswire (bl). **214 Getty Images:** Michael Allio / Icon Sportswire (cra). **214-215 Getty Images:** Michael Allio / Icon Sportswire (Background). **215 Getty Images:** Bettmann (bc/Al Unser); Chris Graythen (ca); Michael Allio / Icon Sportswire (c); Bob D'Olivo / The Enthusiast Network (bc); Focus on Sport (b). **216 Alamy Stock Photo:** Graham Morley Historic Photos (bc). **216-217 Alamy Stock Photo:** Jon Sparks (c). **217 Alamy Stock Photo:** The Picture Art Collection (cra); Jan de Wild (br). **218 123RF.com:** Leonard Zhukovsky (clb). **Alamy Stock Photo:** imageBROKER (crb). **Getty Images:** Jean-Loup Gautreau / AFP (bc). **219 Alamy Stock Photo:** Everett Collection Inc (bc); PCN Photography (cr); Trinity Mirror / Mirrorpix (ftr); imageBROKER (tr). **Dreamstime.com:** Trentham (clb). **220 123RF.com:** Alexutemov (tr). **Alamy Stock Photo:** Lucy Calder (br). **Getty Images:** Manuel Blondeau / Icon Sport (bc). **221 Getty Images:** Nao Imai / Aflo (bc). **222 Getty Images:** The Asahi Shimbun (cr). **223 Getty Images:** Visual China Group (tl). **224 123RF.com:** martinkay78 (br). **Alamy Stock Photo:** Action Plus Sports (bc). **Dreamstime.com:** Vladimir Galkin (bl)

Cover images: Front: Alamy Stock Photo: Action Plus Sports cra; **Dreamstime.com:** Skypixel cla; *Back:* **Alamy Stock Photo:** Cultura Creative (RF) cra; **Dreamstime.com:** Astrofireball cla, Idey cl, Stephen Noakes crb, Oocoskun tc

All other images © Dorling Kindersley
For further information see: www.dkimages.com

DK would like to thank:
Martin Copeland and Lynne Murray for picture library assistance, and Marie Lorimer for indexing.